LET'S
KILL MOM

Berkley titles by Donna Fielder

LADYKILLER

LET'S KILL MOM

LET'S KILL MOM

Four Texas Teens and a Horrifying Murder Pact

DONNA FIELDER

BERKLEY BOOKS, NEW YORK

BERKLEY

An imprint of Penguin Random House LLC
375 Hudson Street, New York, New York 10014

LET'S KILL MOM

A Berkley Book / published by arrangement with the author

BERKLEY® and the "B" design are registered trademarks
of Penguin Random House LLC.
For more information, visit penguin.com.

ISBN: 978-0-425-28037-9

PUBLISHING HISTORY
Berkley premium edition / November 2015

PRINTED IN THE UNITED STATES OF AMERICA

10 9 8 7 6 5 4 3 2 1

Cover art: *Stairs* © by Jill Battaglia/Trevillion Images.
Cover design by Sarah Oberrender.
Interior text design by Kelly Lipovich.

Penguin
Random
House

Dedicated to the memory of my mom,
Nan Campbell, and to all the mothers who have
sacrificed so much for their children.

Acknowledgments

My unending gratitude to law enforcement officers Tracy Murphree, Brian Peterson and Eric Kolda for their willingness to help with facts and details without which this book could not have been written. I love you guys.

I also want to thank law enforcement officers Larry Kish, Jeff Coats, Sharon Baughman and Roanoke Police Chief Gary Johnson for their assistance. It was invaluable. Denton County Prosecutor Vicky Abbott helped me understand the juvenile justice system, and I am grateful.

But the heart of this story is Susan Bailey's mother, who relived the anguish of the events in 2008 so that I might re-create the emotions of a woman torn between love for her grandchildren and grief and anger over the death of her daughter. She is a strong woman, worthy of great respect.

Prologue

Detective Brian Peterson turned the hamburger patties on his grill, enjoying the sizzle of fat dripping on charcoal and the coolness of the breeze on his patio on a late September Saturday afternoon in Roanoke, Texas.

"This has been such a nice day," he told his wife as she brought out iced drinks and buns for their backyard picnic. "It will be my luck to catch a homicide tonight."

"Don't say that! You'll jinx it," she said.

But the jinx was in already. Had been for two days. Before the sun came up the next morning, Detective Peterson would be called to a house of horrors to investigate the murder of a woman whose body had been lying facedown in an upstairs hallway of her home in a quiet, middle-class neighborhood in the little town since the preceding Thursday night. By Sunday, her clothing was dyed black-red in blood, and the carpet under her was sodden and beginning to crust.

Arterial bleeding from her ragged neck had spattered the walls, and the tub in a nearby bathroom contained a butcher knife and three cell phones under a foot of water.

There was poisoned pudding in the house and a baseball bat on a bed. A crude device for electrocuting someone had been rigged in a bathroom. Everything pointed to the woman's own children as the killers.

This was a murder house. It had been set up by youngsters who liked role-playing games and fantasy. But these children hadn't been playing this time.

The woman still wore her name tag from the job she'd left about eleven thirty P.M. on Thursday, September 25, 2008.

Susan, the tag read.

Susan Marie Bailey, forty-three, had died from more than two dozen stab wounds and two slashes to her throat. Dead at the hands of her own two teenage children and her daughter's boyfriend.

"We just didn't see eye to eye," seventeen-year-old Jennifer Bailey later coldly told police about the murder of her mother.

She was dead serious.

1

A Sweet Minnesota Girl

Susan Marie was always laughing, always bubbly and funny and outgoing and smart, her mother, Katherine "Kate" Morten* remembers. She was a towheaded child whose curly hair darkened as she grew older. Susan enjoyed life as the second child in a family of four children, and got along well with her older sister and two younger brothers. As she grew up she displayed musical talent, and played violin in her school orchestra and clarinet in the school band. She spent hours practicing her two instruments. Her mother thought Susan might grow up to be a musician.

The Mortens lived in a suburb of Saint Paul, Minnesota, on a street that dead-ended in a pasture, where horses and cows grazed behind a fence. It was the best of both worlds,

---

* Denotes pseudonym

with the city nearby yet a country feel to the neighborhood. There were only ten houses on the short street. The neighbors all knew one another, and their children played together after school. Susan and her friends learned to play softball in the summer and to ice skate in winter. She formed two lifelong friendships with kids on that street. She was the kind of friend who was always ready to help a buddy in need, no matter how long it had been since they'd last been together.

As Susan grew older, she spent most summer weekends with her grandparents, who owned a lakeside resort. There were rooms to be cleaned, laundry to do and meals to cook. The extensive grounds needed care. Susan helped out with the chores and earned a bit of pocket money there. It was a fun job that included swimming, boating, fishing and playing cards with the guests. Her mother was never sure if she did any real work to earn her pay from her grandparents, but she knew her daughter was safe and happy with them.

By the time Susan was ready for college, she wanted freedom to try her wings, but it wasn't time yet for her to fly away. She enrolled in a local Minnesota college and earned a degree in business and accounting. Susan had a plan. She loved fashion and wanted to work in an area that allowed her to be around pretty clothing. She wanted to work in retail, but she wanted more than just a clerk's job and recognized that to get ahead she needed expertise in the business end of retail clothing. She took her first job in retail with Levi Strauss & Co. to help pay her way through college. That job allowed her to move out of her childhood home and into an apartment with a friend, but that didn't work out well, so she moved back home.

The last winter that Susan spent in Minnesota is remembered by natives as "the big snow." Sixteen inches fell on Halloween, and it kept up all winter. Minnesotans are used to deep snow and cold chills, but this was a particularly difficult and long winter. It was hard for Susan to get back and forth on her twenty-mile commute to work. For months that winter she struggled out of snow drifts and drove through blinding blizzards. She asked for and was granted a transfer to a store a little closer to home, and it was easier after that—but then that spring it snowed another twenty-eight inches. One night she had to close the store, meaning she was the last person out of the building after all the customers had left and the cleaning had been done. She locked the front door and walked to a deserted parking lot. It had been snowing all day, and Susan found her car was covered in a snowdrift in the parking lot of the mall. It was dark and cold, and she was alone. She couldn't even get the car doors open in order to get inside. She was freezing. From a pay phone, she called her parents, shivering and crying, and they brought snow shovels to rescue her. They all took turns digging out her car, and then she followed her parents home.

"I'm never going to spend another winter in Minnesota," she told her mother. And she never did.

Another friend had moved to California, and she asked if Susan would like to come there and live in Riverside with her and her mom. There were plenty of jobs there in the late 1980s as well as fun and sun on nearby sandy beaches.

Yes she did, Susan answered. She craved the sun. Susan wanted to live in a big city and she thought California would be a great place to live.

She promptly packed her car with all her possessions and bought her dad a return airline ticket to Saint Paul, and the two of them drove off in her car to start her new great adventure. That move shaped everything that was to come. Susan was excited. Finally, she could live and work someplace warm and have the independence she craved.

Susan loved clothes. She adored the color pink, and many of her well-put-together outfits incorporated one shade of pink or another. Once in California, she began working in a clothing store, and she enjoyed helping her customers pick out dresses and pants and blouses that suited them. In sunny California she could even sell brightly colored shorts and tops and bathing suits. Soon, she had a following of customers who came to the store just for her. She remembered their names, their sizes and the sorts of styles they favored. She chatted with them about their jobs, their children, their pets. Susan was a natural saleswoman, and her bosses noticed. She was on her way to the career she had dreamed of.

She called her mother often. California was wonderful, she said. There were so many places to go, it was so different—so warm—and she loved the beach. And she had met this man. . . .

Her parents visited once and were introduced to Richard Bailey, who was in the Air Force. He was not as tall or as big as Susan, but he was handsome, with brown hair, dark eyes and a mustache. He was Susan's first real boyfriend and she was obviously in love with him, but her parents weren't too impressed. He was from California and had that "beachy" attitude. He wasn't especially friendly to his girlfriend's reserved northern parents, and they didn't warm up to him. Maybe it was just the uniform she was attracted to, they hoped. Maybe she would find another man in uniform to fall for.

But Susan was smitten.

"Mom, I'm married," Susan told her mother in a telephone call in early March of 1988. "Richard and I eloped!"

Her mother wasn't thrilled about the news, but it was too late to do anything about it. Kate just hoped her daughter would be happy.

Susan also wanted to be happy. But she and Richard moved often as his postings changed, and she was lonely while he was on duty. Just as she would begin to make friends at a base and find a job, they'd relocate and Richard would take off for his next assignment, leaving her alone again. In telephone calls from military posts in Washington, Hawaii and other places, Susan told her mother how Richard called her from ports afar and told her about new friends he was making. Kate didn't know what to make of that. She thought it made Susan jealous, but she didn't know whether or not her son-in-law was actually cheating on her daughter. When Richard's hitch in the Air Force was up, he enlisted in the Coast Guard, but in 1990, after he finished his first hitch, he left the military. They went to live with his parents in San Bernardino, California, and Susan became pregnant with their first child, Jennifer.

Susan continued to find jobs in retail, and she was

successful. Which was a good thing, she told her mother, because once Richard was out of the military, she supported the family. When she became pregnant again four years after Jennifer was born with their second child, David, Richard's father took over child care when Susan resumed working. Kate got the distinct impression that, although Richard's mother was around, she wasn't much help with the kids. But Susan depended on her father-in-law.

In between jobs, Richard stayed at home and helped with the children while Susan worked. Her family time grew shorter and shorter as she advanced and soon she was given her own store to manage in Victorville, California. She was moving up in the Jay Jacobs retail clothing company.

In 1997, Susan was offered another promotion. She had been doing so well that the chain administrators wanted her for more important work. They offered her a position as district manager in the chain for parts of Texas, Louisiana and Oklahoma. She couldn't pass up a promotion like that, so they looked for a place to live in the Dallas–Fort Worth Metroplex that would be central to all of the area she was responsible for. And so they moved to Texas.

Texas is called the Lone Star State, and Texans are proud of their state shrine, the Alamo. Northerners may question why the site of a total defeat by Mexican General Santa Anna in 1836—during which every soldier defending the old mission was killed—would be so beloved, but Texans admire how it inspired others to fight. When General Sam Houston finally defeated Santa Anna, Texas became a republic and adopted a flag that consisted of single red and white horizontal stripes with a blue vertical stripe on the left side. Inside the blue was one white star.

All the drama (and the wealth that later came from cattle ranching and oil wells) engendered an attitude in Texans that persists today. Born-and-bred Texans consider their state and its people a cut above the others, and few newcomers from other states find that attitude amusing.

The Bailey family didn't. They found Texas hot and barren and several cuts below California.

Texas took some getting used to. It was not California, that was for sure. It was miserably hot in summer and often bitterly cold and wet in winter. The seasons of fall and spring hardly seemed to last a week. At first, the family rented a house in North Richland Hills, a suburb of Fort Worth. But Richard and the children hated it there. The tables had turned—now Richard was the one stuck somewhere new without family or friends while Susan was on the road often supervising stores in parts of three states.

The cities of Fort Worth and Dallas lie next to each other in North Texas. Since they're only thirty-five miles apart, one would imagine that they would be similar, but they are actually very different. Dallas is a slick, sophisticated city built on oil wealth. Its more well-to-do citizens project an aura of old wealth and sophistication. Dallas didn't depend on actual oil wells, with their accompanying messiness and smells, but became a financial center for oil, with such tycoons as H. L. Hunt and Clint Murchison making billions off the "black gold" without ever touching it.

Fort Worth, on the other hand, is a city built on cattle wealth. It is a "country" city where men wear gleaming cowboy boots to formal events and may own several pairs but perhaps only one good pair of running shoes. Fort Worth is laid-back and easygoing. It has its well-to-do people and its rich neighborhoods all right, but Fort Worth has a sort of "aw, shucks" attitude that often charms outsiders. "Cowtown," as Fort Worth is nicknamed, retains its bovine panache—every morning and afternoon, Texas longhorn steers amble down East Exchange Avenue in the Stockyards area of north Fort Worth and people gather to watch the real cowboys herd the steers—and influences the area around it.

North Richland Hills, where the Baileys lived, is a solidly Fort Worth suburb, and while Susan was in one of her three-state territories, Richard and the children stayed there and endured. But they were not happy, despite the plethora of activities the area offers. Their home was only minutes from Arlington and Grand Prairie, which held between them the Dallas Cowboys' Texas Stadium, the Texas Rangers' Ballpark in Arlington, the original Six Flags Over Texas theme park, Lone Star Park (a horse-racing entertainment area), a huge water park called Hurricane Harbor and lesser attractions like Louis Tussaud's Palace of Wax, a drive-through wild animal park and the International Bowling Museum and Hall of Fame.

Susan thought the area amusing and picturesque. The rest of her family yearned for California. Besides, the attractions were expensive for a family of four, and with Richard often not working, they took advantage of few of them. Richard and the children read and watched TV, and when Susan wasn't home, they rarely even left the house.

Then Susan found a new housing addition in the little Texas town of Roanoke, which was down US 377 north of Richland Hills and only twenty-four miles from Fort Worth. They bought a piece of property and began construction on a big house. A developer was building out an addition on the north edge of town called The Parks of Roanoke. It was centered around a small children's park and playground where kids could walk from their homes without getting onto any main streets and play in safety. It was quiet, away from the bustling US 377 that ran past the neighborhood, but close enough for commuters to pull out from the subdivision and travel quickly south to the Metroplex area of Dallas–Fort Worth or north to Denton— a university town and the county seat—to work.

Between Denton and Forth Worth, Roanoke and other small towns are strung along the highway like pearls on a necklace. Roanoke, Texas, was a tiny and slow-growing town, and by the time the Baileys moved there in 2000, the population was only about eight thousand people. It started as a settlement of twenty people in 1847, north of the present site in south Denton County, but when the Texas and Pacific Railway came through, the settlers moved south to the railroad station. One of the surveyors named it after his hometown of Roanoke, Virginia.

Early on, Roanoke was a cattle center, with two hotels, two saloons and one house of ill repute, located upstairs from the Silver Spur Saloon on the main street of town. The brothel was reached either by an outside staircase or via a back staircase inside the bank down the street, which led to a secret door to the brothel so men could walk sedately into the bank and back out later with no one the wiser about their real destination.

Sometime over the years, as the railroads became less important to the area, the hotels closed their doors and even the brothel went out of business. But the town eventually sprang back as a bedroom community for the neighboring cities.

Roanoke now lies at the crossroads of US 377 and Texas 114. Both are busy highways. Inside the city limits, TX 114 bears the name Byron Nelson Boulevard after the famous golfer who lived there from after his retirement from the national golf circuit until his death. When Susan needed to drive to one of her Oklahoma stores, it was a short trip to Interstate 35W and another hour down the interstate to the Red River and the Texas–Oklahoma state line. Louisiana was a moderate drive to the east, so the town Susan chose for her home was convenient for her work.

The Texas House of Representatives gave the town the official title "Unique Dining Capital of Texas." In 2014, the town of eight thousand people had forty restaurants to choose from. The old main street of the place, Oak Street, is lined with mom-and-pop restaurants that offer fried chicken, chicken-fried steak, German and Mexican food, fancy hamburgers and Texas barbecue. On weekend nights the population swells with visitors from the Dallas–Fort Worth Metroplex area looking for some comfort food.

Susan loved Babe's Chicken Dinner House. It had opened in 1993 and was the first of a chain of Babe's restaurants in Texas. That first restaurant offered fried chicken and chicken-fried steak, along with fluffy biscuits, an assortment of home-style vegetables and gallons of sweet tea. You ordered one entrée or the other and the waitresses brought the homemade biscuits and vegetables family style for as long as you could eat them. The mashed potatoes and gravy were legendary. Susan loved the food and the décor in the restaurant. Heavy wooden signs hanging from the ceiling honored longtime waitresses. On the exposed-brick north wall hung signs like "Home of Lousy Coffee and Loud Waitresses," and "This Property Is Protected by Fire Ants" (a Texas scourge known to kill cattle and even people on occasion, so the funny sign had some basis in credibility—no one wants to be attacked by fire ants).

Susan also thought it was amusing to watch new customers try to find the bathrooms in Roanoke's Babe's. They were located down a hall that ran alongside the dining area and kitchen, cut into the walls in such a way that you just had to push in a certain place to open them. Small signs designated which one was for men and which for women, but the signs weren't noticeable among the art on the walls. Often a customer set off the emergency exit alarm in search of a bathroom, and when the alarm sounded, the regulars smiled. They knew another embarrassed customer would be shown the secret of the restrooms by an attentive manager.

The Baileys' new home on Oxford Drive in The Parks of Roanoke was worth about a quarter of a million dollars, though Susan and Richard paid under market value to build it because the builder was anxious to sell out the neighborhood. Susan was so excited to watch it go up and then to

finally be able to live in her dream house. It had four bedrooms, two baths, and a large game room upstairs. Downstairs were a formal living room and dining room, a family
room, eat-in kitchen, laundry room and a powder room.
Susan loved her new house and decorated it tastefully. She
made the drapes and curtains herself on her sewing
machine.

The neighborhood grew larger with plenty of families
with children after they moved in, and the brand-new
3400-square-foot house was right across the street from
the neighborhood park. It was the kind of place where the
kids all headed for the park in the summer and after school,
and adults went there to supervise their children and got
to know their neighbors. Susan thought it was just the right
kind of neighborhood for her family. It was away from the
dangers of big-city life. It was quiet. It was safe from the
outside.

Susan had no idea how dangerous it would become for
her on the inside of her own home.

2

The New House

Susan Bailey soon made good friends in the newly built, upper-middle-class neighborhood. Kim Aiken lived around one corner and Sheryl Barnes lived around another. They all had children about the same age, most of them "tweens" or preteens. Sheryl's back gate opened onto the park, and her friendly home became the bathroom-break spot for many of the children who lived too far to run home for a pit stop. Susan's house, across the street from the park, was likewise a good place to take a break if it was too hot or too cold to stay outside for long periods. The three women spent time together in the park or in one another's homes. They became the kind of friends who confided in each other.

Susan had a well-paying job but it wasn't enough. Richard worked, went to school and watched the children, and his dad gave money to help out. But the kids were getting older and they wanted the same kind of clothing and toys the other kids had. The house payments had not seemed large when they took on the big two-story house, but the utilities cost much more than they had imagined. Susan began taking in sewing and started a small home-based business selling Mary Kay cosmetics. Mary Kay is a Dallas-based cosmetics company that had been started by Mary Kay Ash in 1963, specifically as a company where women could succeed. Ash made millions helping other women move up in business, and Susan admired her story. Susan laughed when she told her friends that it was a wonderful job for her, because the company's signature color was pink. The company even gave out pink Cadillacs to their top sellers, and Susan said she planned to have one of those fancy pink cars. After all, she sold a complete line of makeup and facial creams—all of them packaged in a pretty shade of pale pink—she was a good saleswoman and pink was her favorite color.

But all her extra jobs never seemed to bring in enough money, and she wasn't getting along with Richard. She was actually glad when her job took her away from home for a night or two. She turned the large upstairs game room into a workstation for her part-time jobs. All four of the bedrooms were on the second floor, and there were two bathrooms up there. The game room took up a big northeast corner. She put her sewing machine and her sewing supplies there. She made a tiny dressing area with a curtain across one corner for her sewing clients to use to try on altered clothing, and she hung a rod for the dresses and shirts and pants she was altering. Bookshelves lined one whole wall of the room. She turned one group of those shelves into storage for her cosmetics business. There was still room for books and her growing collection of movies, and the other half of the room provided a place for Jennifer and David to hang out upstairs. Both of the kids had separate bedrooms, which Susan decorated with bright colors and airy curtains. Downstairs they had the two living areas, the eat-in kitchen and the dining room in which to watch TV and do their homework. It was a big house. Susan loved it. She loved sewing heavy, elaborate drapes for the formal rooms and bright, happy curtains for the kitchen and the children's rooms. She had an eye for décor.

But all was not well with the family. Jennifer and Kim's daughter often hung out after school until Kim began noticing that often, after Jennifer left, something would be missing from her daughter's room or another part of the house. The next time Kim saw Jennifer, she would confront her about the theft. Sometimes Jennifer apologized and brought back the missing item. Sometimes she simply denied the theft. Finally, the mom had enough.

"You are just going to have to stop inviting Jennifer over," Kim told her daughter. "She is stealing our things and she is not going to stop."

Kim could not bring herself to talk to Susan about the problem. Her friend had problems enough, she thought.

Susan also confided to her friends about problems that she was having with her son, David. Always the smallest boy in his class, he looked and acted much younger than he was. He had an angelic look about him and his mother's sweet smile. But he got into fights, which escalated as the years wore on.

David was also a chronic bed wetter, Susan told her

friends. His room always reeked of urine. He had bunk beds and he sometimes moved from one to the other without changing the sheets. She was sick of having to do the smelly laundry, but she didn't know how to stop the problem. She did not believe the issue was medical and did not seek help from a doctor. (Chances are she was right; doctors who study the issue have learned that bed-wetting, or enuresis, is often the result of a child sleeping very soundly and they'll eventually grow out of it.) Apparently, however, it was a source of deep frustration for Susan and her husband, and David likely felt guilty about something he could not control.

Jennifer told her grandmother once during a telephone call that she had been asleep one night when her father woke her. David had wet the bed, Richard said, and ordered Jennifer to change the sheets. *Why couldn't the boy's father change the sheets? Or why not teach David to do that chore himself?*

When Richard and Susan were both away from the house, their children had strict orders not to make telephone calls or use the Internet. They were to stay in the house with the doors locked. Even though they lived in a very safe neighborhood, Richard had grown up in a part of California where that was the way kids had to act because it was too dangerous to go out by themselves. It made for a lonely life, especially for Jennifer, who wanted to go places and see things and did not want to have to stay home taking care of her little brother. She resented the confinement and she resented being given chores. Her father did little around the house and her mother was tired when she returned from one of her business trips. Duty for the chores belonged mostly to Jennifer, but she often rebelled against what she thought was the unfair division of work around the house. She cleaned only when she was forced to do so, and the house showed it.

Susan's friends noticed that she was growing more and more unhappy. Jay Jacobs, the retail clothing chain where she supervised stores in three states, went bankrupt and closed the doors of all its stores, leaving Susan without a job. She was in a panic, because Richard wasn't working at that time either, and although she quickly found employment managing a nearby plus-size clothing store, Lane Bryant, her salary was greatly reduced from the money she'd formerly made as a three-state supervisor. So Susan began working extra hours in other Lane Bryant stores and later obtained a part-time position in a Bed Bath & Beyond store in addition to her regular job.

She liked working at Bed Bath & Beyond. She didn't have the responsibility of being a manager, and there were so many different home décor items for sale. It was fun helping customers pick out dishes or coffeepots or bedding or the myriad other items the store had for sale. But working that many hours a day wore her out. Susan called her mother often, but most of her talk was about work. She immersed herself in her work, her mother thought, to avoid the unhappiness that was her home life.

Even when something good happened, like when Susan won a cruise trip to the Bahamas for being one of the top sixteen sales managers for Lane Bryant in 2005–2006, it started a huge family fight. Richard wanted to go on the trip, Susan told her mother, but she didn't want him along. Besides, if he came with her, who would stay at home and take care of the children? The yelling got so bad, Kate Morten noted, that her granddaughter, Jennifer, called the police one night.

During this time, Detective Brian Peterson visited the house in connection with a separate investigation and met Susan. He came to know and like her. He considered her straightforward, down-to-earth and honest. Susan eventually filed for divorce, but she cried when she told her friends, and she was depressed when they met for coffee or a soft drink in the kitchen of one friend or another. Susan sought and gained full custody of her children, and in late December of 2006 she was granted a default judgment divorce because Richard never hired a lawyer or showed up for hearings. She was awarded everything in the house, even some of his personal items, because he never asked the court for anything.

After the divorce, Susan worked even longer hours. She worked more part-time jobs. She increased the number of sewing projects she took in and tried harder to sell cosmetics. Her growing children needed more and more expensive things, and the big house was consuming her bank account. Richard was required to pay child support, to be taken out of his pay before he received any money, but despite his payments Susan still struggled to make ends meet. In the meantime, Jennifer was beginning to complain about having to be David's "mom." She became more and more resentful, and the two often argued. The teenager didn't seem to understand that her mother was forced to work so many hours to keep food on the table and pay their bills. Teenage girls often resent their mothers and talk back to them, but Susan told her friends that Jennifer's attitude was wearing on her.

The issues with David hadn't eased either. He was very

intelligent, his mother said, but he didn't apply himself to his studies, so his grades were not good. And there were behavior issues. He could be charming and outgoing but he also seemed to fight a lot. By the time he was attending middle school, the fighting seemed to be getting worse. And his teachers noticed signs that he was a "cutter." "Cutting" is referred to by authorities as self-harm. It includes scratching or making shallow cuts on the skin, usually the arms, and often cutters suck on the wounds. Cutting is commonly believed to be a symptom of borderline personality disorder, depression, anxiety, low self-esteem or a history of emotional or sexual abuse. David, they noted, was making cuts on his arms.

Susan worried about David, but she did not seek psychological help for her son. He seemed to be getting more and more out of control. He was in trouble at school a lot. She wondered whether his behavior was connected to the divorce. Richard was no longer in the picture and the children were often alone because she needed to work so many hours.

Still, she spent as much time with both her children as she could. The family had always been avid readers. They made frequent trips to bookstores, and the whole family read the Harry Potter fantasy books together. When the movies based on the series came out, they saw them as a family. She often took Jennifer and David to movies, and she bought hundreds of DVDs for them to watch at home. They even went to the Six Flags Over Texas theme park.

Still, she knew she needed to spend more time with her children.

She tried.

3

The Journal

In 2006, Kate Morten, Susan Bailey's mother, began keeping a journal. Her life was full and busy, but she still had time to herself. She thought it would be fun to chronicle the life she and her husband, Stephen*, lived in Arizona during the winter. It was so different from their Minnesota life, where they now ran the same tourist resort on a lake that Susan's grandparents had run, and were hosts to fishermen and people who just wanted to get away for a while. In Minnesota, Kate cleaned cabins and washed sheets and cooked meals while Stephen worked on their boat and the cabins and kept the yards nice. But in the wintertime, in Arizona, they could rest and socialize, and Kate would have time for writing. It was good to spend those months play-

---

* Denotes pseudonym

ing games and talking to the friends who always showed up from other cold climes. It would be fun to write down all the things that happened in the snowbird village.

They traveled the miles between their two homes twice a year and also made road trips from both locations. Kate enjoyed her "snowbird" life in the warm state in winter and wanted to be able to remember the details when she became too old to carry on with all her activities. So Kate bought a pretty, hard-backed, loose-leaf book with the word "Journal" and pink, red and yellow flowers on the front. She began writing on October 18, 2006, as she and Stephen were packing to leave for their winter in Arizona. She wrote about quilt making, visits with neighbors and relatives and trips to the doctor. Her posts were infrequent and recorded the somewhat mundane life of an older couple with many friends and close ties to their relatives. She recorded that they'd made side trips to Branson, Missouri, for a Crystal Gayle concert and to the Ozarks on their way down to Arizona to see the fall leaves. They arrived and moved into their winter home. They went to a clinic for flu shots, made dinner for friends and played bingo. Her grandchildren, Jennifer and David, flew in for Christmas in December 2006. Kate thought they were sweet kids, and she enjoyed having them. Her daughter had stayed in Texas that year to finalize her divorce from Richard while the children were gone.

"Good for her!" Kate wrote. "He was rotten."

The journal went on, Kate noting distant relatives who had died and a fashion show she participated in. In late January 2007, she fell, badly bruising some ribs. She was so sore, she wrote, that Stephen had to tie her shoes for her.

They made a trip to California in February. She was making a quilt for one of her grandsons' graduations but had been so busy she hadn't made much progress. In March she acted in a funny play about nuns called *Bad Habits*. Later that month she wrote that she was eager to return home to Minnesota. It was ninety degrees where they lived in Silveridge RV Resort, near Mesa, Arizona, and she was ready for some cooler weather. There was a going-home party at the retirement community and she hung her beehive quilt on the wall as a party decoration and bought fresh daffodils for the tables. The Mortens said their good-byes to their winter friends and set off for Minnesota. They arrived home early in April to very different weather. Kate wrote that their sewer had frozen solid, and it took Stephen several days to thaw it out. In late April, they got eight inches of snow.

There followed a hiatus of nearly a year in journaling. Then, in February 2008, Kate wrote that she had found her journal and would begin writing anew. She was back in Arizona, and the entries were full of fun with her winter friends. But the entries were sporadic, and in April she wrote again about going home to Minnesota, where about twenty-two inches of fresh snow greeted them. There was little written that spring. Then, on June 22, 2008, Kate wrote that they were on their way to Susan's house in Texas for Jennifer's high school graduation. They arrived about ten P.M. and both Jennifer and Susan were working. That would be the rule during their visit, and Kate was disappointed that she was not able to see much of her daughter. Susan was buried in her work, Kate wrote. Kate was unhappy about that. It seemed to her that Susan should have taken at least one day off to spend with her parents.

From this moment on, the tone of Kate's journal entries changed—instead of short, happy, sporadic entries from a woman clearly too busy enjoying herself to find time to write much, the diary became a place where Kate wrote lengthy entries about stressful, tension-filled encounters with her daughter and her grandchildren.

Instead of a fun record of her adventures, the diary became a chronicle of Kate's journey through hell.

4

Paul

Jennifer Bailey was a pretty girl at seventeen, of medium height with long light brown hair, straight eyebrows above her hazel eyes, a sweet smile and a nice figure, though for her first three years in high school, she never had a real boyfriend. She wasn't especially outgoing or particularly popular and didn't run with a crowd of girls, but neither did she ever get into any trouble.

Not until she met Paul Henson.

Jennifer was taking Spanish her senior year and floundering with it, so she went to Susan's friend and neighbor Sheryl Barnes, who was fluent in Spanish, and asked for help. Sheryl agreed to tutor her, but time was a problem. Finally, Sheryl found a solution. She began driving Jennifer to school each day, and during the drive they spoke only Spanish, with Sheryl correcting Jennifer's mistakes. The tutoring helped. Sheryl thought Jennifer was a sweet girl.

But then Jennifer started dating a boy named Paul Allen Henson Jr. He was a grade below her, and they didn't live particularly near each other, so having actual dates was difficult. Jennifer had not obtained a driver's license, and Paul had recently obtained a permit but didn't have a car. They discovered the distance wasn't too far to travel on their bicycles, so they visited at each other's homes while their parents were at work and met at other places where they could be alone.

Both teens attended Northwest High School, which lies in far southwest Denton County. When Sheryl wasn't driving her, Jennifer rode the school bus to the campus in the town of Justin. Paul lived just outside the city limits of the small nearby community of Haslet with his father and stepmother.

Paul's parents were divorced and his father had full custody. Paul Henson Sr. had filed for divorce from Paul's mother, Terri Ann Henson, in 1995 when Paul was three years old. At that time, Paul Sr. was forty-one and Terri was thirty, according to the divorce documents. His occupation was listed as cab driver and hers as unemployed. Paul Sr. hired a lawyer and the case went to court in Denton County. He asked for the house in Haslet, both vehicles, all the furniture and full custody of Paul Jr., whom he called "JR." The reason given for the breakup of the marriage was the standard "discord or conflict of personalities." Terri did not retain a lawyer and did not contest the divorce or custody issues. When the divorce was final, she was given standard visitation and ordered to pay one hundred dollars a month child support.

Paul Sr. eventually remarried, and his son lived with the new couple in the same house in Haslet where they had lived with Terri. Haslet had a population of only about fifteen hundred, and eighty-five percent of its residents were white. The town's area is only about eight square miles, but it straddles the county line between Denton and Tarrant counties. In 2008 the median income was ninety thousand dollars a year, though the Hensons likely were not in the ninety-thousand-dollars-a-year income bracket. They lived in a mobile home community called Songbird Estates, situated in a mixed neighborhood of trailers, manufactured houses and businesses. A long gravel drive led to the white-and-gray Henson trailer and a pole barn. There was also a pond on the property.

Paul was sixteen when he and Jennifer began dating. He wore his thick, bushy hair and bangs long, and they overpowered his face, which was less than handsome. His bangs met his eyebrows and his unruly hair was down on his shoulders. His two front teeth were large and protruded slightly. He was over six feet tall and at only 145 pounds, he looked thin. Peering into his blank dark eyes was like staring out a window on a black, starless night. But Jennifer looked into those eyes and saw something that others couldn't fathom.

His friends told odd stories about him. He had a split personality, they claimed. His "Paul" personality was mild and slow to anger. But his friends said that he also had another personality he referred to as "Thomas." (A later investigation showed that Paul actually named his other personality "Talos," but apparently the strange name confused his friends, who thought he was saying "Thomas.") This other personality was aggressive and prone to violence. One of his friends claimed that Paul once told him that "[Talos] is going to kill if I let him out."

The teenager also had a fascination with vampires, his friends said. He wanted to be one, and he claimed that he was the reincarnation of an executioner who'd lived in the eighteen hundreds.

Paul was known to have severe mood swings and sometimes spoke or chanted in some kind of unknown language as though he were speaking to someone no one else could see. Most people thought all this was just an affectation he used to get attention—especially from girls. He wasn't especially good-looking, but he seemed to do well with the opposite sex. There was something about his dark eyes, some people thought, maybe something strange that peeked out occasionally.

Jennifer had always been a reader, and she loved fantasy books. She and Paul had a lot in common, they discovered once they started hanging out together, and Susan was vaguely aware of other interests the two shared. They were both into "emo," emotional hardcore music based in punk rock. Emo appeals to disaffected kids who feel they don't fit into traditional society, and its followers are rumored to be into activities like bloodletting, experimentation with same-sex intimate relationships, depression and suicide. Like most parents, Susan thought her daughter's choice of music was less than melodic but she never really listened to the words.

Jennifer and Paul also sometimes ran with a group of

kids who played Dungeons & Dragons, a complicated fantasy role-playing game that's been around since 1974.

Those who play often fancy themselves smarter than the average young person because of the complex rules and the amount of imagination and cunning it takes to play. Numerous books on the subject help players learn how to assume the roles of knights, bards, thieves, monks, necromancers or even the dungeon master—the player who runs and referees the game—and to magically traverse catacombs under castles, ride horseback across kingdoms and use medieval weapons to kill their enemies.

Players gather around and take on a role or character they make up. The characters go on imaginary adventures together, fighting monsters and various other bad elements. It's a young person's game, with interest usually starting in middle school and extending through college. The games last for hours, and can continue for days, weeks, or even months or years. The game likely was the beginning of Paul's supposed second personality, Talos the executioner.

Jennifer appeared to be fascinated with the game and with Paul's other role playing. She also wrote fanciful plays that she and Paul acted out. Her character was named "Lilly." Then she became interested in witchcraft and told her friends she was a Wiccan. The Wicca belief stems from the saying "an it harm none, do as thou wilt," meaning that one can do as one pleases as long as it harms no one. Wicca means "witch," but followers claim to use witchcraft in a good way. Jennifer's friends didn't know whether she really believed in the religion of Wicca or if she just had fun with some of the more dramatic things Wiccans did. She talked about reincarnation. She seemed to think that she and Paul had lived prior lives together. They began wearing dog collars with each other's names on them.

This behavior worried her mother. Susan didn't like Paul. She thought he was strange, and she hoped that Jennifer would find someone else to date. Instead they seemed to grow closer, and Susan and Jennifer argued over the relationship. The arguments escalated as Jennifer's senior year wore on.

And then another girl entered the picture, and Susan didn't understand that at all.

5

Merrilee

Merrilee White* was a pretty girl with black eyes and long brown hair that she sometimes lightened to a reddish blonde. She came from an affluent family in the far northwest part of Fort Worth, an area that lay within the Northwest Independent School District. Her mother and stepfather were divorced, but he still functioned as a father figure in her life. She lived in a home worth more than a quarter of a million dollars, and she also attended Northwest High School. Merrilee was fourteen years old and a freshman the year that Jennifer Bailey was a senior and Paul Henson Jr. was a junior.

Normally, older teens would not befriend someone that

---

* Denotes pseudonym

young. But Paul liked Merrilee. He began hanging out with her when he was not with Jennifer. Amy White*, Merrilee's mother, didn't like Paul at all. He had an unattractive overbite, he looked unkempt with his long bushy hair and something in his eyes concerned her. He seemed to have a lot of strange ideas. Her daughter's relationship with the boy worried Amy, and she forbade Merrilee to see him anymore. The girl ignored that.

Paul was mysterious and exciting to Merrilee. Merrilee went right along with all that stuff about previous lives and she started listening to emo music as well. She looked into Paul's dark, somewhat vacant eyes and saw a romantic character from her own fantasies. She knew that he was involved with Jennifer and was jealous. But Paul told the two girls that he had a split personality. He explained that he was actually two males in a single body but they were not the same person. His "Paul" personality was in love with Jennifer, he explained. But his other personality loved Merrilee. Both girls bought his story.

He had sex with both girls, and before long he had brought them together. Paul convinced Merrilee that Jennifer was special, and when the two girlfriends became friends with each other, Merrilee was thrilled to be part of the threesome. She'd never really had a best friend, and the two girls became close. And then they became even closer. Merrilee had experimented with lesbianism with another

---

* Denotes pseudonym

girl at school. Soon, the three had sex together, with the two girls becoming sexual partners as well as having sex with "Paul" and "Talos."

Merrilee once complained to a friend that she was angry with "Talos" because "Paul" was having sex with Jennifer and suddenly became "Talos." Her boyfriend cheated on her with Jennifer, she said.

When Paul and Jennifer started including her in their get-togethers, they all decided that Merrilee also had been with them in prior lives. Therefore they all belonged together and would remain together for eternity in one life after another, but they had to stay together in each life too, they decided.

Such was the relationship that spawned a murder pact.

6

Graduation

It was the end of the school year in 2008, and Jennifer Bailey was graduating from Northwest High School. That and her upcoming birthday in October were her keys to freedom, she thought. She'd be out of school and eighteen years old—an adult, finally. She had a cute outfit for graduation, and both she and her boyfriend, Paul Henson Jr., had new clothing for the senior prom. He wore a suit without a tie and she wore a rose-colored beaded gown that her mother had made for her. She pulled her hair back and up and looked pretty. Both of them looked nice in their official prom portrait. But there was something about Paul's eyes that came through in the picture. A Texas Ranger later said that you could look in the eyes of the pair in the prom photo and see that something bad was going to happen.

Jennifer wanted to attend the Art Institute of Dallas after graduation. She wasn't a great student, but she had some artistic talent that she wanted to further, and she thought this was a way of achieving higher education and turning her talent into a tool for getting a job. She badly wanted to be out on her own, but she knew she'd have to find a way to make money to accomplish her dream.

Susan was working long hours trying to save money for tuition to the school. It was costly to attend, and money was tight as usual. She eventually took out a loan so that her daughter could get the education she wanted. She paid tuition for the first semester and made plans to take some vacation days late in September to go down and enroll Jennifer in the school. But first they had to get through graduation. And that wasn't as easy as it sounded.

Susan loved her daughter and wanted her to be happy. That seemed to be a harder task than it should be at that point. Jennifer wasn't cooperating with much of anything, and she and Susan argued often, mostly about Paul. Jennifer also missed her dad and wanted him to be at her graduation. Susan doubted he would come. David played games on the computer and watched TV. He didn't want to get involved in the arguments.

Susan's parents, Kate and Stephen Morten, and one of her brothers came down from Minnesota for the graduation ceremony. They came early, and Kate was home with Jennifer and her brother, David, after school while Susan worked. But Kate wanted to see her daughter. She resented the fact that Susan didn't take any time off for their visit, just continued to work every day, getting up early and returning home late. Kate had rarely been able to spend any time at all with her daughter because of the distance between their homes, and now that she had made the trip, she wanted to visit. But Susan said she could not take any days off of work. She needed the money now more than ever, she said, because she somehow had to find the where-withal to buy another car for Jennifer to get back and forth to school. (Jennifer still didn't even have a driver's license, but that was another hurdle down the road.) Susan worked hard and fretted and paid little attention to her parents during their visit. Kate sat and stewed and wondered in her journal why they had even bothered to come all the way down to Texas.

One Saturday, when Susan was at work, Jennifer begged her grandmother to pick up Paul at his home just across Texas 114 in Haslet and let him spend the day. Stephen and their son were off exploring together, leaving Kate at home alone with the two teenage grandchildren. That didn't make the grandmother happy either, but Kate agreed. Haslet was easy to get to; Texas 114 bridged the two major highways between their towns and made it possible for Jennifer and Paul to visit each other by riding their bicycles, or sometimes by hitching rides. And with their parents at work and Jennifer's little brother, David, pledged to secrecy, it was easy enough. But on this day there was another way for them to be together and Jennifer begged. Kate wanted to please her granddaughter, so off they went to fetch Paul.

It didn't take long to find the mobile home and collect the boy, but by the time they got back home, Kate was already wishing she had not agreed to bring him to Roanoke. She thought Paul seemed strange. He was all "handsy" on Jennifer, and just as soon as they arrived back at the house in The Parks of Roanoke, the two teenagers disappeared upstairs. Kate didn't like that. Maybe they were in the game room, but she could hear no noise from up there: no television, no sign of any activity. She grew more concerned as time wore on and decided to investigate. She climbed the stairs and turned left to the first door, which she knew belonged to her granddaughter. Jennifer's bedroom door was locked. Hesitantly, and then louder, she knocked on the door. After a short wait, Jennifer opened it, wearing only a hastily pulled-on shirt, and Kate suspected that she was naked underneath it. Jennifer said Paul was in the bathroom, but Kate could see the open bathroom door just down the hall, and he was not inside. She kept asking, louder and louder, more and more upset, and finally Jennifer said he was in the game room. Kate stepped to the doorway and saw him pulling on his pants. Kate was aghast.

She ordered both teenagers to get dressed and come downstairs. It took them a while but they finally descended into the living room, not looking Kate in the eye.

"I am taking Paul home," she said sternly. "Get in the car."

Jennifer argued and cried, but Kate was done with the two. Silent, with her mouth in a tight line, she drove Paul back to Haslet and told him to get out of her car. Jennifer didn't speak to her grandmother for the rest of the day and was pouty and morose during the rest of the visit. Kate was so angry that she didn't care. She was responsible for her granddaughter, and she had done something nice for her. Jennifer had repaid her by having sex with her boyfriend right in the house with her grandmother downstairs. It was disgusting. And she felt like her daughter should know what was going on between the two. After dinner, after Jennifer went up to her room, Kate told Susan what she had seen. Susan didn't say much. She just shook her head and went upstairs to talk to her daughter, then she came back downstairs and they watched television. Susan didn't tell her mother what had happened in Jennifer's room. The topic just did not come up again, and Kate left it alone. She decided it was her daughter's business, and if she didn't want to talk about it, well, fine. Kate had a good idea though that Susan had thoroughly chewed out Jennifer, and that was good enough.

Jennifer was also upset because she wanted her father to attend her graduation and she had not heard from him. Would he come all the way from California, or Iowa, or wherever he was, to see his only daughter graduate? Jennifer didn't know and she moped around the house waiting for him to call. Jennifer threatened to stay at home that night rather than graduate without her father there. *That girl was such a trial. She ruined every celebration with her histrionics,* Susan told her friends.

Richard finally called to say that he was in Texas and would be coming to the ceremony. Jennifer perked up and began helping to make plans for attending her graduation. Kate was surprised. She had not known that her former son-in-law had returned to Texas and was living nearby. Susan may have known, Kate thought, but she never told her mother much about private things. (In fact, Richard Bailey had at first not told his children that he was back in Texas for reasons he did not divulge to his former wife.)

Kate knew there were plans for a small reception after Jennifer's graduation but saw no work had been done toward having company. She went to the store and purchased groceries and began looking up recipes for refreshments.

Susan left for work one morning with orders for the children to clean the house. Jennifer was to vacuum. The carpet was dark in heavy traffic areas and clogged with dog and cat hair from the family pets, a basset hound named Ginger and a cat whose name Kate didn't know that hid when visitors came. Both apparently were prolific shedders. Later that morning Kate asked Jennifer whether she had vacuumed and Jennifer said yes. But Kate could see all the pet hair covering the floor and the furniture and knew that was a lie. Instead of challenging her granddaughter on the obvious fabrication, Kate began vacuuming over Jennifer's cries that she already had done that chore. The vacuum bag quickly filled up, and Jennifer emptied it for her grandmother without a word. Kate did not lecture her granddaughter about the lie because she was trying to maintain some kind of happy atmosphere. She just wanted some peace in the house she was visiting. She finished the job herself and Jennifer went back upstairs to her room.

Susan always asked her daughter to clean and Jennifer never did it, Kate thought. She could see that nothing her daughter did or said seemed to have an effect on Jennifer's behavior. Susan tried being nice, she tried yelling, she tried leaving notes with lists of chores on the refrigerator door with a magnet. None of them moved the girl away from the television set or the books she read constantly. Kate believed her granddaughter's passive-aggressive attitude was her way of rebelling against having to watch her brother while her mother worked. *Jennifer was a troubled girl*, her grandmother worried. David was pleasant to his grandparents and never seemed to cause trouble.

Later that morning, Kate decided to call a truce. She went upstairs to talk to her granddaughter. She asked her what her plans were after graduation. Jennifer quickly replied that she wanted to move out. Jennifer clearly fancied herself put-upon and neglected. She was sick of taking care of her little brother, she said. She was sick of being told to clean the house. She had a friend who would let her come and live with her. She wanted to be on her own. So Jennifer thought she wouldn't have to clean house when she moved in with her friend? Kate thought. They would see how that worked out.

"I don't know how she thinks she will live on her own," Kate wrote in her journal that night. "She thinks she's neglected at home. Weren't we all at that age?"

Friday, June 27, 2008, dawned and Jennifer was happy. Her father was coming to the graduation ceremony. Richard was not traveling from Des Moines, Iowa, where she had thought he was living, the girl told her grandmother. He was just over in Arlington, less than thirty miles away. It would be no trouble at all for him to drive over. Susan left for work and Kate began early preparation for the party food. Susan had told her they were having a few neighbors over but Jennifer told her grandmother that she had not invited any friends there. Those two just didn't seem to communicate at all, Kate thought.

Susan left work early for once and arrived back at the

house at eleven A.M. They decided to give Jennifer her graduation presents. Stephen, Jennifer's grandfather, had made a beautiful cedar chest for her. Kate had picked out blown-glass dolphins that she thought would remind Jennifer of California and the ocean she loved. Susan gave her pearl-and-gold earrings and a necklace to match. They were lovely. For once, Jennifer seemed happy and excited. She dressed nicely for the ceremony and looked really pretty, her grandmother thought. David had a suit to wear as well, and he hijinksed around the house in his fancy duds.

The family drove in two cars to the graduation ceremony at a large university auditorium in Denton. There were eight hundred students in Jennifer's graduating class and no auditorium in any of the Northwest School District buildings was big enough to hold all the people who would attend. So, like most high school graduation ceremonies in the area, Jennifer's took place at the University of North Texas Coliseum. Kate noticed that Jennifer's boyfriend, Paul, and a man she assumed was his father were sitting across the aisle from the Baileys and the Mortens. Susan said she hoped there wouldn't be any trouble; she thought Paul Sr. did not like her because she discouraged Jennifer from seeing his son. Paul's dad, on the other hand, liked having Jennifer around because she "calmed [Paul] down," Susan said.

Jennifer disappeared briefly after the ceremony and her mother panicked. She ran around the huge building looking for her daughter, who turned up a few minutes later from the opposite direction. Kate thought she had been with Paul for a few stolen moments, but the girl shrugged off questions from her mother after she made her way back to the family. Things were a little tense while they tried to take family photos, but they finally left for home so they could start the open house. Neighbors stopped by with cards of congratulation for Jennifer. Richard had arrived as promised, and he came back to the house as well and stayed awhile, taking some of his tools and other property from the garage when he left. All in all, Kate thought the graduation had gone fairly well. But she was glad to be going home the next day. All the tension in her daughter's house was exhausting.

7

David

Kate and Stephen Morten would not be returning home to Minnesota alone—earlier in the visit, Susan had asked her parents if David could spend the summer with them. She was working long hours and Jennifer had recently obtained a job at a nearby fast-food restaurant, and Susan didn't want thirteen-year-old David to spend too much time by himself.

He had never really had the time to get to know his grandparents, and she thought it would be good for him to bond with them and to work a bit around the resort, as she had when she was his age. She also knew that he would enjoy time spent at the lake. He would have a good summer and his mother would not have to worry about him.

Kate was hesitant to take on her grandson, but she agreed to try the arrangement for a month. He drove away with them, leaving only Jennifer for Susan to deal with all summer.

And that was not an easy task. The formerly sweet girl who'd loved her mother had turned into a sullen, mouthy teen who acted as though she hated her. Mother and daughter continued to fight over Paul. When Susan forbade her to see him, Jennifer moped around the house hugging a teddy bear he had given her. Once the two teens ran away together, but they soon were caught and brought home by Paul's dad. More than once Jennifer disappeared and spent the night at Paul's house, and his father brought her home in the morning after discovering her in Paul's room. There was constant tension and bickering. Jennifer and Paul found a place online where people could register themselves as married, and they did that. Susan was beside herself. She did not like this boy!

Susan e-mailed her ex about the issues she was having with Jennifer and Paul, but Richard didn't have any good ideas about keeping them separate. The situation was spiraling downward, she wrote him. But Susan was too busy and too exhausted to do much about it.

In the meantime, while Susan was busy working her two jobs, Jennifer and Paul continued to hang with Merrilee when she could get a ride to Paul's or Jennifer's house. Paul's father and stepmother also were gone at work all day, and Paul's house was much closer to the part of Fort Worth where Merrilee lived.

Back in Minnesota, things went well at first. Kate wrote in her journal on Tuesday, July 1, 2008, that Stephen was getting David outside and teaching him to do things the boy had never done before. He taught his grandson how to do some of the chores around the lodge. He taught him to fish. David seemed happy and was talkative and outgoing. He was afraid of the water, but after one of his cousins came to visit he began swimming in the lake. He wanted a snorkel, he told his grandfather, and Stephen indicated that might happen. When Kate took David to the small nearby town one day, he thought she was going to buy a snorkel for him. Kate didn't. He got angry and protested that she was supposed to buy one for him. It was his grandfather who promised him a snorkel and it would be his grandfather who would have to get it for him, she explained. Suddenly, David turned into a different boy; his face contorted and he began yelling. He was nearing violence, and Kate had to stop the car on the way home to try to calm him. She had never seen David like this.

"You need to respect your elders," she admonished.

"What about you respecting me?" was the answer.

Kate realized that the boy had no respect for his elders. But by the time they arrived at the lodge David was over his anger, and his grandfather took him fishing. It was astonishing, she thought, and a little scary, how fast David could change from good spirits to near violence and back again.

David read a lot while he was in Minnesota and his grandparents thought that was a good thing. They took him to the local library often. One night his mother called and Kate heard him tell her that he loved her. That made Kate happy. Maybe it had been a good thing after all for him to come to Minnesota with them.

Then Kate noticed a sore on David's upper thigh. She thought it was a boil. She put hot packs on it to bring it to a head and finally, it opened. But the material that came out was bloody and green and sickening, and when it was cleaned a large gaping hole remained. Kate was scared. She didn't have David's insurance card. Susan was supposed to send it but it had not come in the mail yet, and she did not have written permission to seek medical attention for her grandson. She called a nurse who told her to keep the wound clean and it should heal. One of David's cousins then developed a similar sore. His mother took him to a doctor and learned that the sore was a staph infection. He had "caught" the infection from David. And now David had another lesion on his arm. And the next day yet another appeared on the same arm. The day after that, David's insurance card finally arrived along with a permission note from Susan for his grandparents to see to his medical care. Kate called her doctor but his appointments were full that day. Another sore appeared. Kate tried to keep them clean and get them to heal but David kept picking at them, no matter how much she told him not to. She finally was able to get him into the doctor's office. A nurse took a culture, and Kate learned that the sores were a strain of staph called MRSA, a bacterial infection spread by skin-to-skin contact or contact with a surface someone infected has touched. This strain cannot be cured with most common antibiotics, and in some instances it can be fatal. Kate cared for David's lesions and watched him carefully to keep him from pulling or scratching at the sores. She did not send him home after a month. She believed he needed careful treatment and knew that he would not get the attention he needed at home.

Jennifer seemed upset about David staying longer,

perhaps jealous of the attention he was getting from his grandparents. Suddenly, she was angry at her brother and would hang up when he tried to call her. That upset David, who was really attached to his sister. Susan didn't understand why her mother wanted to keep him longer. Kate thought that her daughter just didn't understand the seriousness of the infection. Susan wouldn't be staying home to take care of him, and Kate believed he needed that kind of care. Susan finally sent an airplane ticket and told her mother to just put him on the plane. Kate did as her daughter asked, worrying all the while.

David was excited as he kissed his grandparents good-bye and boarded the plane. His sister had called to tell him there was a surprise waiting when he got home. It was a cellular telephone with a data plan. He could play games and even watch TV on it. Jennifer had one too. And then there was his dad, who finally was paying him attention. Richard came by one night after his son's return from Minnesota and picked him up for a movie date. David was happy to have his father to himself because Jennifer didn't want to go. Her whole focus was on Paul, her boyfriend. She wasn't allowed to go out with him, but she would rather stay at home and talk to him on the telephone than spend time with her father. That after making such a fuss about Richard coming to her graduation.

Jennifer's plans were to start attending the Art Institute of Dallas early in October. Susan had arranged to take vacation days at the end of September to get her enrolled in the school and oriented on the campus. Susan was trying to work a deal to give Jennifer her car and buy a newer one for herself, but she didn't quite have the funds for that. Jennifer wanted to live in Dallas, but Susan certainly didn't have the money for an apartment and upkeep. Jennifer would have to live at home. She was angry about that and said she didn't want her mother's old car either. Why couldn't she have a new one? she asked. Soon, Susan realized she wasn't going to be able to swing a car payment anyway. She talked to Jennifer about riding the train to college. There were stations convenient to the school and to Susan's place of work. Jennifer could ride in with her mother and then board the train the rest of the way. But Jennifer was going to attend evening classes and didn't want to ride the train at night.

Nothing seemed to please her. Jennifer was hostile. She wanted things she couldn't have and she didn't want to compromise.

Susan had been happy when she purchased each of her children a cell phone and put them on a family plan with her cell. She didn't know that while she was at work Jennifer spent all her time on the phone gobbling up their free minutes and then using big chunks of pay-per-minute time, and that David overused Internet data. Her first telephone bill was a shocking fifteen hundred dollars. Then a notice came from the bank. Jennifer's checking account was two hundred dollars overdrawn.

"I can explain," Jennifer told her. "My paycheck is late, and I didn't know it was going to be and wrote some checks. I can get the money in the bank as soon as I get my check from my job."

Susan went to the fast-food restaurant herself and asked about her daughter's late paycheck. The manager explained that Jennifer didn't have a check coming. She hadn't even worked there for the last six weeks. She'd just stopped showing up.

Then one day while she was at work, Susan got a call from Roanoke police. David had been running around the yard naked and the neighbors called to complain. Susan was horrified and deeply embarrassed. She promised that would never happen again. But how could she prevent it when she was working most of the time? Would it ever end? Yelling at David didn't seem to stop his strange behavior. Yelling at Jennifer didn't discourage her from her relationship with Paul. The problems were dizzying, and she had no help solving them.

Kate called to see how things were going on Tuesday, September 23, 2008. She spoke to Jennifer, who told her grandmother how upset she was about her mother asking her to ride the train back and forth to school in downtown Dallas. She didn't want to ride the train at night, Jennifer complained.

"So you expect your mother to get out at night and drive to downtown Dallas to pick you up?" her grandmother asked in exasperation. She just could not fathom her granddaughter's selfishness.

"Gotta go, Grandma," Jennifer said, and hung up the telephone.

It was the last time Kate would talk to her granddaughter for a long, long, time.

8

Runaways

Police believe that Susan Bailey had houseguests in late September 2008, though apparently she was not aware that anyone other than herself and her children were in the house. She was working two jobs at the time, managing a Lane Bryant store and also working at a Bed Bath & Beyond store in Hurst. She was likely too busy and exhausted to notice clues that, at least part of the time, other people were staying in her house.

Her daughter's boyfriend, Paul Henson Jr., had run away from his parents' house in Haslet, and Paul's other girlfriend, Merrilee White, had also sneaked away from her home in Fort Worth. Both were hiding in the big Roanoke home. When Susan was at home, they slipped into the unused extra bedroom or behind Jennifer's closed bedroom door or into her closet. Sometimes they hid in the park across the street from the Bailey home. They had the run of the house when Susan left for work, and she was gone most of the time. They played their fantasy games and had sex. Jennifer wrote plays and they acted them out. They ate the food Susan brought home and left the kitchen a mess. David knew they were in the house but he climbed on the school bus every morning and said nothing to his mother about the kids hiding there.

Police believe it was during that time that the teens began perfecting a plan they had talked about for some time. None of their parents wanted them to be together. Both girls' mothers had ordered them to stay away from Paul, and Paul's dad was tired of all the drama and had told him to stay away from Jennifer too. It was getting more and more difficult at their homes, and the teens were convinced that they had to stay close to be together in their next reincarnations. What they had to do, they decided, was get rid of their parents. Kill them. All of them.

But Jennifer's mother had to be first, they decided. She was the worst. She yelled at her daughter and made threats about sending her to Minnesota to live with her grandparents. She might just do it too; David had stayed there all summer. Jennifer wasn't going to Minnesota. She just would not do that. Susan had to die, she told her teen lovers. Her mother *had* to die.

The teenagers spent hours talking about ways to do it. She could make some pudding and put a big load of some kind of prescription medication in it, Jennifer said. If she crushed up a whole bottle of pills, that should do the job. Her mom liked chocolate pudding. She'd eat it.

What about electrocuting her in the bathtub? Paul

suggested that if they plugged in an electrical cord and put the other end in the tub when Susan was in it, she would die of electrical shock. He said he'd seen that in a movie. If they took the cord away afterward, maybe the cops would just think she'd had a heart attack. Or maybe they should hit her over the head. David had a small wooden bat his grandfather had carved for him. They could use that. Maybe they could knock her unconscious and roll her into the tub and then put the cord in the water. That seemed like it might work. They were full of ideas. They would run away to Canada. All of them would go, they decided. Even Merrilee and David. Jennifer didn't want to leave her little brother, and he wanted to go.

They talked it over and decided on how the other parents would die. Paul's dad had a .22-caliber Ruger pistol. Paul decided to steal it and then wait for his father and stepmother to come home one night and shoot them both as they came in the door. It would be simple. Merrilee should stab her mother in her sleep, they decided. It wouldn't be hard for Merrilee to catch her mother sleeping and get her out of the way. She was just as bad as Jennifer's mother, really, and she would never allow Merrilee to go to Canada with the other two if she were alive. Merrilee would do it, she said. No problem.

Merrilee had left home on Friday, September 19, 2008, and her mother, Amy White, reported her as a runaway. Amy knew that Merrilee and Jennifer Bailey had become close friends and thought that maybe her daughter was at the Bailey house in Roanoke. She called Susan that Friday night to ask if her daughter was visiting in her home, and

Susan (who didn't know differently) said no. When Merrilee did not return to her home in Fort Worth by Monday, September 22, Amy drove to Roanoke to place posters in public areas asking people to call if they saw her daughter. She spotted Merrilee walking alone from a Walmart store near The Parks of Roanoke neighborhood toward the Bailey house.

Amy made Merrilee get into her car even as the girl protested and cried. At first she tried admonishing her daughter. Then she tried reasoning with her. Neither worked. Merrilee was angry and defiant. She was so out of control by the time they arrived at their home that Amy called police. Fort Worth officers responded and talked to both mother and daughter.

One Fort Worth officer took Merrilee out to his squad car and helped her into the passenger seat. He wanted to talk to her without her mom being present. Merrilee just sat there crying. The officer asked her why she was so unhappy.

"Because there is nothing anyone can do once things get started," she said. The officer told her he didn't understand. Could she explain?

"There is nothing anyone can do. If things start they are going to happen."

The officer told the sobbing fourteen-year-old that he could help if she would allow him to help. He asked her to explain what she was talking about.

"There is nothing you or anyone can do to help me," she said.

Then she told the officer that her "baby" had broken up with her. He finally managed to get her to tell him that her "baby" was Paul Henson Jr. but she wouldn't say anything else about him. The officer took her back inside, where another officer had been talking to Amy White. The two officers tried to persuade the mother and daughter to talk to each other, but Merrilee refused to talk to her mother. They did extract a promise from her that she would not run away again, and since no crime had been committed and Amy did not want to press runaway charges, they left.

Merrilee went up to her room. She seemed a bit calmer. Amy went to bed, but it was hard to sleep with her unhappy daughter in the next room crying.

The next morning, Tuesday, September 23, Amy got out of bed and found Merrilee awake. Recognizing that she had been through a great deal in the past few days and that she also seemed to be coming down with a cold, she asked the girl if she would like to stay home from school. Merrilee said yes. Amy told her that she would work from home that day and they could spend some time together and talk things out. The mentally and physically exhausted mother decided to get a little more sleep before she began her work and dozed off. But she soon awoke with a strange sensation that something had bumped the bed. Sleepily, Amy turned over and opened her eyes.

Merrilee was hovering over her mother with a big knife in her raised hand.

Confused, frightened and angry, Amy quickly backed off her bed away from Merrilee and grabbed her cell phone. She called 911 for help. The 911 recording later showed that Amy told the dispatcher her daughter was threatening her with a knife. Amid muffled crying and shrill comments from Merrilee in the background, Amy could be heard yelling, "Put that knife down! What the hell do you think you are doing? Throw it down!"

The dispatcher quickly radioed two officers to head to the house.

"Give me your cell phone and the car keys," Merrilee could be heard screeching at her mother. "I have to go with them!"

"I'm not giving you my car. You are not driving," Amy told the fourteen-year-old.

"We were all supposed to go. And you ruined it!" Merrilee screamed.

After some muffled outbursts and sounds of scuffling, Amy reported to the dispatcher that she had the knife. The dispatcher told her that officers were on the way and she would let them know that the situation had deescalated.

Officers arrived and Amy opened the door for them. She was shaking. They again talked to her and her daughter separately. Then they took Merrilee to juvenile detention and charged her with aggravated robbery. But since she was a family member and someone who lived in the house it would be hard to prove a case of robbery. So later the charge was changed to aggravated assault, family violence. The near-hysterical girl was placed in a juvenile cell, where she cried herself to sleep.

Merrilee remained in the juvenile detention center for several days. On Wednesday, September 24, 2008, Fort Worth police learned that Merrilee's boyfriend, Paul Henson Jr., was also a runaway, and that he had taken his father's gun. Paul Sr. filed a runaway report on Tuesday and other agencies learned about the gun from the report. (Paul's plan to kill his parents one night had backfired as well, he'd told both of his girlfriends earlier. He'd gone home and waited for them to get home from work, but instead of coming home right away, Paul Sr. and his wife had decided to catch a movie and have dinner out. That movie saved their lives. Paul waited as long as he could stand it, then, bringing the gun and a box of .22-caliber ammunition along with him, he caught a ride back to Jennifer's house.) The officers didn't know this yet, but they were concerned because Paul's father had told them that his .22-caliber Ruger pistol was missing, and because there was a rumor that Paul Jr. had made threats against the high school he attended. If Paul had his father's gun, it meant he had the means to carry out those threats. That was serious enough that officers decided to interview Merrilee to find out what she might know about any plan to start shooting at the school. They obtained her mother's permission to question her, and two detectives went to the detention area where she was being held that Wednesday afternoon.

They took Merrilee to an intake office for the interview, and a juvenile officer remained in the room with them. They explained to her that Paul had run away from home after ransacking it, and had taken a pistol and ammunition with him. What did she know about that?

"If Paul has a gun, the plan is in motion," she said.

What did that mean? the officers asked her. If he had a gun he could be hurt, or he could hurt someone else.

"The plan is in motion for them to get a car and go to Canada."

Who was "them"? the officers wanted to know.

Paul and Jennifer Bailey, she said.

One of the officers contacted his superior on his radio with the information. The other officer replied that a Roanoke officer had been to the Bailey house and no one was at home. There was a rumor that Paul had fled to San Antonio. The officer with Merrilee told her what he had learned.

"But the plan was to go to Canada," she said.

Fort Worth and Roanoke police exchanged information. It was clear that there had been some sort of plan to be carried out, and Merrilee was part of the pact. It was chilling. By the time they found out just how horrifying the conspiracy actually was, it was too late to save Susan Bailey.

9

Meanwhile in the Bailey House

That same Tuesday, September 23, 2008, when fourteen-year-old Merrilee White hovered over her mother with a butcher knife, was also an eventful day at the Bailey house. Thirteen-year-old David Bailey had arrived at school with a knife. Some kids saw him showing it off, and one of his friends tried to hurt another boy with it. Some of the other students told their teacher, who told the principal. David's locker was searched and the knife was found. He was given a three-day in-school suspension for possessing the knife and school officials notified his mother. Instead of going to class, David would have to stay in an office with other youngsters who had broken school rules, under direct supervision from a principal, his mother learned. He brought home a document explaining the suspension and Susan used a magnet to attach it to the refrigerator. She would have to deal with it later, she supposed.

Paul Henson Sr. had also reported his son as a runaway that Tuesday. Paul Jr. had been home part of the time and missing at other times, but his father had not contacted authorities until that morning. He told the Denton County sheriff's deputy taking the report that the teen most likely was with Jennifer Bailey, and recommended that her house in Roanoke would be a good place to start looking. Though the Henson mobile home was near Haslet, it was technically outside city limits in unincorporated Denton County. That was sheriff's office jurisdiction.

Henson Sr. originally filed the runaway report with Roanoke police, and they forwarded it to the Denton County Sheriff's Office. The runaway information, including the details about the stolen handgun, were placed in reports sent to all county agencies. Unless they are urgent, reports from one day are given to detectives the next morning. Sheriff's Investigator Don Britt read the runaway report in his office on Wednesday morning and called Paul Sr. Nothing had changed since he filed the report on Tuesday, the father told Britt. His son was still missing and he suspected the boy was at his girlfriend's house. He gave Britt directions to the house in The Parks at Roanoke, and Britt decided to drive over there immediately.

Don Britt was a veteran detective with the sheriff's office. While detectives there worked all kinds of cases and were not specifically assigned to any type of case, he had become the go-to detective for runaways because he'd had some success in finding them. And if there was a girlfriend or boyfriend in the picture, that home was the first place he always looked.

Looking for runaways is not a particularly pleasant task. Everyone is upset, and the kids are often wily about hiding. Parents who demand that their children be found then often do an about-face when the officer rounds them up. Running away is a juvenile offense, but the parents most often become angry if their kids are detained. They just want them home, and once they are returned, the parents often just want the officer to go away. It's a thankless job. Some detectives rely on the natural order of things when assigned a runaway case; most of the time, kids come back on their own when they run out of money or hospitality at their friends' homes. But Britt was a bulldog. Once he got a case in his teeth he didn't want to drop it. He believed he had sort of made a job for himself by searching so aggressively for runaway kids. So his sergeants had come to rely on him to find the kids and relieve the parents' minds.

Britt parked in front of the Bailey house on Oxford Drive in The Parks of Roanoke before nine A.M., hoping to catch Paul before he had a chance to get out of the house. Susan Bailey answered the doorbell.

No, she said, Paul Henson Jr. was not at her house. He was not allowed to visit, and she would know if he was there. No one was at home besides her and her two children. Despite what Susan said, Britt figured the boy was even then hiding under somebody's bed—most likely Jennifer's. Susan admitted that she worked nights at her second job most of the time, and that it would be easy for a teenage boy to sneak in and hide when she returned home late at night. But she did not believe that had happened. He asked if he could talk to Jennifer. Susan invited Britt in and called her daughter downstairs. Britt saw a pretty, petite teen with long swinging light brown hair, slowly descending the staircase. Jennifer didn't seem happy to see him. Her face looked like she was trying not to show any emotion.

"I'm looking for Paul Henson," Britt told her. "He's been reported as a runaway and his father thinks you might know where he is."

"I don't know," Jennifer muttered. "I haven't seen him since Saturday."

Britt didn't believe her. He thought she knew exactly where Paul was at that moment, and he suspected Paul was somewhere in that very house. Britt asked Susan if he could talk to Jennifer alone, but the mother didn't like that idea. She seemed protective of her daughter, and Britt had no legal opening to insist on a search and upset her at this point. So he questioned the uncooperative girl a bit longer, but Jennifer was not giving him any information. Britt finally decided he was wasting his time at the Bailey house and climbed back into his car. Runaways usually turn up in a day or two, and Paul probably would return home, Britt knew. Still, he was sure that Jennifer knew much more than she was admitting. He didn't like letting the case go, and he followed up on a couple more leads without success before turning his attention to his several other cases. Something about this runaway report and his visit to the Bailey house nagged at him, but he had done all he could do at the time to find the boy.

Roanoke police also were looking for Paul that day. Through police-intelligence channels the Roanoke officers learned that a Denton County runaway might be hiding in a house in Roanoke and he likely had a gun. Two officers and a sergeant responded to The Parks of Roanoke that evening. Paul saw the squad cars arriving about seven fifteen P.M. and slipped out the back door and around the house. He then sneaked into the park across the street.

Susan was surprised to see another officer standing at her door that day, but she allowed Roanoke Officer Alan Moody inside. A second officer, Jason Jones, went to the back of the house but saw no one. Jones returned to the front of the house and went inside. Moody's voice recorder preserved their voices as he, Susan and Jennifer discussed the situation. By this time Susan was angry and Jennifer was defensive. Susan was weary of having police at her door, but she still did not believe that Paul was in her house.

Due to their concerns about the gun, the officers told Susan that they needed to search the house, and Susan agreed. Something was going on that she did not understand, she realized. She and Jennifer continued to bicker over Paul, and their voices were picked up by the officer's voice recorder.

The officers recorded their whole stay at the Bailey house that evening. The recordings reflected the conflict between mother and daughter and the strain Susan was under.

"I knew something was up," Susan's voice was shrill on the recorder. Then, ". . . You have had it so easy! You have all the freedom you want . . . I don't know what the hell is going on!"

Moody and Jones searched the house for Paul. A third officer, Sergeant George Wise, helped and also kept his eye on Jennifer, who he thought was a mouthy teen. The officers didn't find Paul, but they did find packed suitcases in Jennifer's closet.

Sergeant Wise also found Jennifer's cell phone in her room. Notifications showed that it contained voice mail messages that had not been listened to. Wise took the telephone downstairs and asked Jennifer for the four-digit code that would unlock the message device. The girl stalled, but finally she told him. Wise unlocked the messages and listened to them, hoping to hear something from Paul about his whereabouts. There were four new messages, and one saved one. The first message was from a woman who said her name was Amy White. She said she was Merrilee White's mother and she had some information for Jennifer. She asked her to call her back. The second message was from the same woman. Amy sounded as though she were crying on this message. She said she had had a confrontation with her daughter, Merrilee; she quoted a telephone number and asked Jennifer to call her back and tell her whether she recognized the number, which she had found on Merrilee's cell phone. Jennifer had not listened to or returned either call.

The next two messages were from Paul Henson Sr., Paul's father, asking Jennifer to call him because he was trying to find his son and he believed that Jennifer would know his whereabouts. The girl obviously had not paid attention to his concern. Two parents were worried about their children, and both believed that Jennifer knew where to find them. It seemed to the sergeant that more was going on here then they knew, but the teen was not talking. Susan was worried too.

But not worried enough, as it turned out.

The officers continued to search the house. They found a sixteen-inch butcher knife hidden under a couch cushion in the family room. Why on earth was a big knife concealed in the couch? Susan was shocked and Jennifer claimed not to know how it got there. Was someone planning violence? That reminded Susan of a bowl of chocolate pudding Jennifer had made for her. It had tasted nasty, and Susan had only eaten the one bite. Now she accused Jennifer of poisoning the pudding. The girl played innocent, and said the milk had smelled bad and must have been spoiled. They squabbled more in voices not intelligible on the tape. There had been a lot of tension in that house, the officers thought later, though of course they had no way of knowing what was going to happen on Thursday.

The Roanoke officers found a pair of men's shoes and a wallet under a mattress in the game room upstairs. The wallet contained Paul's driver's license, a little cash and a note from Jennifer. One of the officers handed the note to Susan but didn't notice what she did with it. Jennifer insisted that Paul had merely dropped his belongings off at the house on Saturday while Susan was working and that she had not seen him since.

Moody tried to build rapport with Jennifer, talking quietly and calmly to the girl. But Susan was really upset, and she kept interrupting.

"So you and Paul were going to run off again?" she yelled. "I have half a mind to ship you off to your grandmother! You can go to the north woods and play with the raccoons and the bears."

Jennifer swore she knew nothing about a gun.

"We know you are lying," Moody said. "If he has that gun and something bad happens, it's going to be on your conscience."

She didn't know anything about that, Jennifer insisted. She had not seen a gun.

"I told you he was bad news!" Susan interrupted. "You have three choices. You can go to California to your other grandparents, or you can go to Minnesota, or you can go live with your dad."

Even as she said it, the officers doubted that Susan meant it. The statement had the sound of an empty threat, and they suspected it wasn't the first time the threat had been made. Susan insisted that Jennifer bring the suitcases downstairs. She wanted the officers to search them.

"She was definitely leaving," Moody's voice could be heard on the recording as he shuffled through one of the suitcases.

"She slept in her clothes last night," Susan interjected. "She was up all night."

"I just couldn't sleep," Jennifer told her mother.

"No lying!" Susan shouted.

One of the suitcases belonged to Jennifer and was stuffed full of her clothing. But the angry mother was especially interested in the gray, hard-sided suitcase that she had never seen before.

It was packed with male clothing, probably belonging to Paul. There were four knives in there. Susan asked the officers to destroy the knives. She didn't want them in her house. The officers agreed. The gray suitcase also contained some of Susan's books and a large number of her DVDs. Susan became even more upset. Jennifer had not only planned to run away, she was stealing from her mother. And her mother knew that she was lying.

"Those are his clothes," she said. "You want to tell us another fake story?"

The search for Paul concluded and the officers left. Susan called the boy's father, and he agreed to come to Roanoke to pick up his son's belongings. Paul Henson Sr. paced Susan's floor with his face in his hands when he realized how bad things had become. He was especially worried about the missing gun. It had not turned up in the search. Did that mean that Paul Jr.—or "JR," as his father called him—was out somewhere packing heat?

Included in the clothing that Paul Sr. recognized were a jacket and a pair of shoes. His son owned only one pair of shoes, Paul Sr. said. Was he running around someplace barefoot? While Paul Sr. watched, Susan pulled all the clothing out of the suitcases and discovered the magazine from a pistol, loaded with .22-caliber bullets, and a box with some loose ammunition. If the cartridges were in the house, the gun must be there somewhere, the parents reasoned. Susan called the officers and asked them to return. But while another search still did not turn up the Ruger, Officers Moody and Jones did find another big knife under Jennifer's bed and they found a bottle of Zoloft antidepressants in Jennifer's purse that had been prescribed to a Merrilee White.

At that time, the name Merrilee White meant nothing to the Roanoke officers.

Paul Sr. took the ammunition and his son's belongings and left, and another tense evening at the Bailey house wound down for the night.

On Thursday, September 25, Susan reported to the home store after her regular shift at the dress shop. It would be another late night. She had few days completely off, since she worked at one store or the other, or both, every day of the week. But she needed to pay off the huge telephone bill, and she was already planning ahead for the upcoming Christmas. Besides, she had arranged for a few days off soon so that she could get Jennifer enrolled in the art institute. She would get some rest then.

On Thursday afternoon, Susan tried to call Jennifer, then David, to check on them while she was at work. Neither answered, and she left messages that were never returned. *Why wouldn't they answer their phones?*

She confided to a work friend that she was worried about her kids. So many bad things were happening and she couldn't seem to control her children. She was so tired, she couldn't think or plan, and she felt like her life was spinning out of control, she said, appearing deeply worried. She had to find a way to get Paul Henson Jr. out of their lives. *What on earth are those kids up to now?*

They were up to a lot, it turned out. At the Bailey house, the kids were busy setting traps for Susan. The poison pudding had not worked, but Paul thought they might be able to take her unaware and push her into the bathtub and zap her with an electrical cord. He carefully cut off one end and frayed the wires, then draped the cord over the shower curtain rod and wrapped it around the closet doorknob and left it hanging with the prong end near the electrical outlet. He partially filled the tub, just in case. If they could get Susan in the tub, they could pull the cord into the water and electrocute her that way, he explained. Then they could hide the cord, and people would think she'd had a heart attack.

Jennifer placed the small baseball bat that her grandfather had made on her bed, handy if they needed to knock her mom out. David had been in on the secret for some time, and he was on board. It was just like in the movies, he said. He was excited and giggling about possible scenarios. They all picked out knives as weapons. When their mother called, they were too nervous to answer. They might give something away. She was working late at the home store that night, and they settled in to wait for her to arrive home. When they heard her car door bang shut, their hearts began slamming in their chests. It was going down.

10

Murder

Susan Bailey drove the eighteen miles from the Bed Bath & Beyond home store in Hurst, Texas, where she worked a second job, to her house in Roanoke and pulled into the garage. She was angry and a little scared about why neither of her kids had answered their cell phones that evening nor returned the messages she'd left for them to call her. There had been so much trouble that week, and she just wasn't ready for any more.

It was nearly midnight. Susan had helped close the store and was due back the next day. She climbed tiredly out of the car and opened the door between the garage and the main rooms of the house. All the lights were out, even on the second floor, where the bedrooms were. *Had the kids turned in? Were they even at home?* Nothing they did would surprise her anymore. She had ordered them to be awake when she got home. She was taking their cell phones away.

She should have known better than to buy the phones and add the kids to her usage plan. But she wanted to be a good mom, and it was something she'd thought she could do for them without spending a great deal of money. Well, it hadn't worked.

She turned on the living room light. All her nice furniture, cluttered with discarded clothing and dirty dishes. Her beautiful dining room, with its glass-fronted cabinet containing her shining crystal and china and her heavy antique table and chairs; the table was littered with paperwork from a project she was trying to finish. Clothing was draped across some of the chairs. And there was her pretty yellow-and-red kitchen with its cute rooster décor. That kitchen was a mess. Looked like the kids had left the milk out again.

She worked such long hours and she was so tired all the time. . . . The kids just wouldn't help, no matter how much she yelled. Sometimes it didn't seem worth the effort. She had always kept a nice house, but now she just didn't have the energy to do it herself. Or to stand over them while they did it.

She reached the foot of the stairs. No sound from above and no lights had come on when the door slammed shut. She switched off the living room light and turned on the dim light above the stairwell. She reached the top step and turned left, toward the bedrooms.

A strong arm grabbed her around the neck from behind. She tried to scream but a hand clamped over her mouth and a strong chemical smell enveloped her. Suddenly she was surrounded by people. In the dim light she could see her children, but they were wearing kerchiefs tied around their faces. *What?* She twisted hard to her left and was momentarily free of the strong hands.

"Jennifer, call the police!" she yelled. But her seventeen-year-old daughter shook her head.

"No," Jennifer said.

"*No?*"

Panicked, screaming, Susan struggled against the arm that closed again around her neck. Then the blows came. She was dazed, but she kept shouting for Jennifer to help. Instead, Jennifer stepped forward with a knife in her hand and began hitting her mother in the chest, stabbing her. Susan felt a deep, sharp pain low on her back, and her legs crumpled under her. On her knees, she saw the teenagers all around her.

Oh God! Her children were killing her! Why?

The strong hand pulled the knife across her throat and blood spurted from Susan's neck, painting the wall across from where she now fought for her life. She tried to plead with Jennifer and David but could only make gagging noises as she struggled to breathe.

She couldn't move. The teens were shouting now, encouraging one another. Her daughter's boyfriend, Paul, was the one who had come from behind her. He put his face close to hers. She tried to turn her head away but they were almost cheek to cheek as he pulled the knife across her throat again.

Kate's Journal

Friday, September 26, 2008, 4:30 P.M.

Get call from Roanoke police. David not in school that day—Jennifer not at work for 6 weeks. They went by the house—no activity—they must be all together. Why are you bothering us???? Because it is unusual. Susan didn't call to say & didn't show or call at work. Worried and waiting.

11

"I Can't Reach My Daughter"

It was Friday, September 26, 2008. Kate Morten was worried. Someone from the Texas store where her daughter worked part-time had called her mother in Minnesota. Susan hadn't reported for work that day, and she'd never even been late before. The Bed Bath & Beyond home store manager had called her home telephone number several times but no one answered. He had also called Susan's cell phone, but it appeared to be turned off. If she wasn't coming in he needed to find someone to work in her place. He needed to know if she would be in the next day. Kate's number had been listed on Susan's job application as an emergency contact. Did she know where her daughter was?

Kate did not. She'd talked to her grandchildren earlier in the week, she said. But it had been several days since she talked to Susan. Kate knew her daughter well. This was not like her. She always answered her telephone or called right back. Her work ethic was impeccable. She didn't just miss work and she certainly would have called if she were ill.

Kate promised the manager that she would call her daughter, but she got no response from either number either. She left a message but received no callback. Kate did not have Jennifer's cell phone number, but she called David's phone and it appeared to be turned off. *What the heck?* She remembered that she had talked to Jennifer on the house phone on Sunday and the girl told her she was still working to help pay off the huge telephone bill that she and David had run up. She had sounded contrite about that.

Kate tried several more times, becoming more nervous each hour. *Where was Susan?* She always answered her cell. She always returned Kate's calls. *Was she sick? Had there been an accident?* Kate worried more and more. It was hard being so far away. Her other children lived close by and she saw them all the time. But Susan lived thousands of miles away. She couldn't drive to her daughter's house to find out what was wrong. All she could do was worry and wait.

Kate wanted to call the police, but she was confused about all those small-town jurisdictions. She remembered that David went to school in a town called Trophy Club, so she called the Trophy Club police. The Baileys didn't live in that jurisdiction, she learned. But an officer gave her the number for the Roanoke police, which was the police department that would need to check on Susan's welfare, the officer told her. One of those Roanoke officers would go to the house and determine whether something was wrong. So finally, Kate dialed the Roanoke, Texas, police department. She explained the situation and asked if an officer could go to her daughter's house and find out if anyone was at home. *Yes ma'am*, came the answer from the 911 call taker. *I'll send an officer over there right away.*

At 1:36 P.M. on Friday, September 26, 2008, Officers Shane Norman, Annette Meadows and Jimmy Hutchison all drove to the house in The Parks of Roanoke. They knocked several times but no one answered. These were not the officers who had responded to the house searching for Paul Henson Jr. earlier in the week. They were not aware of possible trouble at the residence. There were no lights on in the house, and no movement could be seen through the windows. The car that Susan drove, a blue 2002 Saturn, was not in the driveway and, despite it being daytime, there were outdoor lights shining over the garage. It looked as though no one was at home. The officers left the house and signaled the dispatcher the code for "unable to locate."

A "welfare concern" tag was placed on the address, and other officers drove by. Officer Alan Moody returned about six fifteen P.M. for another welfare check. He had been one of the officers who responded in the search for Paul, but there was no immediate sign of trouble, and he did not connect the empty house with the runaway report. He was uneasy but there was not enough information at that point to do anything further. Nothing had changed from earlier in the day. The outdoor lights were still on and the blinds still were closed. He filed another "unable to locate" report. These things happened all the time. A family left on a trip and forgot to notify relatives. The relatives were concerned but embarrassed for calling police when they learned that everything was okay. There was nothing outside to warrant making entry into the house.

Roanoke officers talked about it at shift change. Kate had suggested they contact her grandson, David, at school, but an officer had visited the school and had learned that David was not in attendance that day. Kate also told them that her granddaughter Jennifer worked at a local taco restaurant, but a call there elicited the fact that the girl had not worked there for a month and a half.

Maybe the family had decided to take a trip. The car wasn't there, and the outside lights were on. The house seemed deserted. But it was strange that Susan Bailey had not told her mother or anyone at work about a trip, and none of them were answering their cell phones. If she was taking David out of school, Susan should have notified authorities in the district. There was a general unease about the family and the situation. Still, they did not have enough information to warrant entering the house without permission from the owners.

Kate called the Roanoke police again. She was worried that something had happened to Susan inside her house. She didn't want David coming home from school and walking into something horrible. When the officers told her that David had not been at school that day, it only worried her more. Where were her daughter and her grandchildren? Something was wrong, Kate knew it. She fretted and worried and tried to think of something else she could do.

The night shift commander told the officers patrolling that section of Roanoke to swing by occasionally to check on the house and see if anyone came home. No one did. The house remained deserted and the garage lights remained lit.

Roanoke police continued the routine of checking the house in The Parks of Roanoke all day Friday and Saturday. Nothing changed. No one moved behind the darkened windows. The outside lights remained on. No car ever pulled into the driveway. A sense of unease grew stronger in some of the officers' minds. *Where were the Baileys?* Roanoke was a small town and it wasn't often that a whole family went missing.

Kate's Journal

Saturday, September 27, 2008

[Store manager] called—Susan didn't show or call for work again today—have we heard from her—he is worried. Said she left work [Thursday] night upset, couldn't get ahold of the kids on the phone. Had trouble at the house she confided in him—with the boy. Assumed it was David's streaking in the front yard.

Called Roanoke police again. Said Susan was no-show at both jobs & no call in not like her to be irresponsible.

Police called back no car at house. Did walk around. No one at home. They didn't notice a dog in the house—thinking maybe they are on the road with the dog. Call house again and leave message hoping to hear soon—it's getting night.

Sunday, September 28, 2008

Get call from Roanoke police want to know if Susan knows anyone in South Dakota. Said no! Where in the heck did that come from? Said they would be in touch. Eased the worry a little bit.

12

Yankton, South Dakota

It was about halfway through the eleven P.M.–to–seven A.M. overnight shift, and nothing much had happened when Yankton, South Dakota, Police Officer Eric Kolda pulled up behind a blue Saturn at the gas station at about three thirty A.M. with his overhead lights flashing. It was a cool night in late September, brisk, and he was wearing his light patrol jacket. He could see what looked like three people in or near the Saturn. The gas station was closed at that hour of the morning, but the car was pulled up to the pumps and someone was outside near the front door of the station. It looked like a teenage boy to Kolda.

As he neared the Saturn, Kolda turned on all his front lights, including a spotlight that lit up the scene. Kolda deduced that the other front-seat passenger was a teenage girl, and he thought it must be a child and a dog in the backseat. Yankton had a teen curfew of eleven thirty P.M., and these kids were out way past that. Besides, what were they doing hanging around a closed gasoline station? The license plate was from Texas. Teenagers a long way from home, for sure. Something about it all set off an alarm in his head. Kolda radioed his location and prepared to leave his squad car.

The boy outside the car looked over at him, walked back to the Saturn, climbed in the driver's seat and slowly pulled away from the pumps. Kolda stayed in his squad car and followed, and after about fifty yards the car with the Texas plates stopped. Kolda radioed in that he was leaving his car and grabbed his big flashlight.

Kolda loved working overnights, what some officers called the graveyard shift. Some officers hated it and found it boring; others liked it because it tended to be quiet and uneventful, and all they had to do to earn their pay was drive around and answer the occasional call. But Kolda valued the overnight shift because it was the best time for crooks to be afoot. He believed that an officer could work as much or as little as he wanted on the late shift. If you kept alert, if you checked into everything that seemed even a little off, if you followed your gut, you could find crimes being committed that others might not notice. Kolda made a lot of work for himself, but he also made a lot of arrests. He loved police work.

Yankton didn't divide the workload into sectors. An officer could patrol anywhere he or she liked, and Kolda always looked for the places where something shady might be going on. Kolda was a hometown boy, and he knew the neighborhoods well. Yankton, the county seat of Yankton

County, South Dakota, lies on the Mississippi River on the border of Nebraska and, with a population of 14,500, is the principal city in the county of only 22,600.

Kolda approached the blue Saturn on the driver's side and looked in the windows. The teenage boy he had seen by the gas station was driving. A girl about the same age sat in the passenger seat, and a much younger boy occupied the backseat, and yes, that had been a dog he had glimpsed when he pulled up. All three kids were dressed in light clothing—too light for the crisp South Dakota air. A few pieces of clothing were scattered around the floorboards. He asked the boy, who said his name was Paul, for his driver's license. It was a learner's permit and very new. He directed Paul back to his patrol car and told him to get inside. Paul would not make eye contact with him, and said very little in answer to his questions. Kolda radioed in yet again and asked for backup. He just didn't have a good feeling about this contact at all.

As soon as other units arrived, Kolda moved Paul to one of the other squad cars, then put the younger boy, who said his name was David, in another and brought the girl, Jennifer, to his own car and helped her into the passenger seat. In answer to his preliminary questions, the girl told him that they were on the way to their grandmother's house in Minnesota. Their mother had sent them up there because she was having financial problems, Jennifer told him. The boy's learner's permit had identified him as Paul Henson Jr., sixteen, of Haslet, Texas. He had an odd, hacked-off haircut that looked fresh. The girl handed over a Texas identification card that gave her name as Jennifer Bailey, seventeen, of

Roanoke, Texas. She had no driver's license. The young boy was her thirteen-year-old brother, Jennifer said. He had no identification. The dog's name was Ginger.

Kolda thought the girl seemed to be acting younger than her years, and she spoke with an innocent, childish voice. But the officer wasn't buying that voice. The girl made his hackles rise. The whole thing felt like an act. Too sweet. Too young-acting for her age. Too innocent. Something was off about her and this whole situation.

Kolda just had a bad feeling. He didn't like the story. He didn't like the vibes coming off these kids. The girl had long, straight, light brown hair that looked tangled from riding a long distance with her head on the headrest. They all looked tired and their eyes, though sleepy, were strange. Nervous vibes came off all of them, and none of them would look him in the eye.

Kolda checked out Paul's learner's permit with the police dispatcher and learned that the boy was listed as a runaway who was possibly in possession of a stolen gun. He ran a license plate check and learned that the car was registered to Susan Bailey, forty-three, of Roanoke. Susan was her mother, Jennifer said.

Kolda recorded his conversation with the girl. He sounded kind and concerned on the recording, but in actuality he was suspicious as hell. Jennifer swore she was telling the truth. She prefaced every other sentence with "I'm not gonna lie," and every time she said it Kolda believed she was lying. It had been his experience that liars often used such phrases to back up their stories.

He questioned her about hanging around the gas pumps. Had they been trying to steal gas? She admitted that they'd been squeezing all the handles to check for a pump that might accidentally have been left on. They were nearly out of gas.

What the heck were they doing in Yankton? Kolda asked.

Their mom had sent them to live with their grandparents in Minnesota and they were on their way, Jennifer said, not explaining why her boyfriend was along. Her mom was having financial problems and couldn't take care of them, so they'd left two days ago, she said.

It was a weird story. *Who would send children by themselves across several states to live with grandparents, with a dog but no luggage? No money?*

"We are flat broke right now," Jennifer told Kolda.

Kolda asked for her mother's telephone number, and Jennifer gave it to him. He called it, but no one answered. He tried several more times with no good results. Jennifer gave him several excuses, but none of them sounded true.

Kolda had wanted to be a police officer since he was twelve. He had been in the military, stationed at Lackland Air Force Base in San Antonio, Texas, in fact. He had been a police officer for several years. Though Yankton was not a high-crime town, Kolda had seen enough to tell when someone was not telling the truth. This girl was lying. Big-time. Something was very strange about the situation with Susan Bailey.

On the recording, the officer now sounded skeptical. *Did their mother really know they were gone?*

"I've been honest. We are supposed to be gone," Jennifer claimed.

There was another lie, Kolda thought.

Jennifer said she was worried. "I've been trying to call Mom to check on her, and she's not answering."

So she had been calling her mother ever since they had been gone with no answer. *Why would her mother not be answering the telephone?* he asked. Jennifer said she thought maybe the phone at her mother's place of work had been acting up lately. *A business telephone not working?*

Why was she worried about her mother? Well, she wasn't answering her cell phone either, Jennifer said. She always answered her calls. But she also claimed that her mother had a former boyfriend named "Joseph," who Jennifer explained had been stalking her mother. She thought "Joseph" might have harmed her.

Kolda was not buying this tale.

"Jennifer, your story isn't matching up. Let's get on with the truth—let's get it all out."

But the girl stalled. Jennifer told him she had been born in California and she missed living there. She didn't like living in Texas, she said. The house was rarely comfortable. Her mother wouldn't turn up the heat in winter or the air conditioner in summer, to save money on electricity. She only saw her dad once a year at Christmas, she said. They talked more, with Kolda urging her to just tell the truth. Her story just didn't add up, he said. *Why would her mother not answer either of her telephones? Why would she send them so many miles away alone?*

Jennifer finally admitted that Susan Bailey did not

know they were gone. They had taken the car without her knowledge.

"We were going to call her and let her know where we are," she said.

Kolda asked, "Did you sneak out?"

"Yes."

"Does your mother have another car to go to work?"

"No."

"Where was she when you left?"

"She was upstairs."

Kolda was concerned when dispatch told him about the possible .22-caliber pistol in the car. The communications officer told him that Paul was suspected of taking his father's gun when he left. So Kolda had searched the car, but no pistol was found. *Where was the gun?* he asked Jennifer. *Was it in the car?*

"There is no gun in the car."

"Where has it been used?"

"I have no idea."

Kolda told the girl that they were going to take the dog, Ginger, to the pound so she would be safe while they sorted out the situation. He was concerned about the things Jennifer was telling him, he said.

Kolda talked to her about her little brother, David. *Why was a boy so young along on this trip?* he wanted to know. Jennifer explained that they were very close, and she'd asked him to come. *What about Paul? Why was he here? Why was he coming with them to stay with their grandparents?* Jennifer began crying.

"He is in so much trouble!"

As she and David left Roanoke, Jennifer said, she'd spotted Paul walking on the side of the highway. She told him to get in the car, and he just came with them.

"You're not making this up?"

"There's no way."

"This is the biggest hunk of fake I've ever seen," the officer said in disgust. "Or the biggest pile of manure." *The way they are acting*, he thought, *their mom is dead.*

Kolda and the other officers took the three teens to the Yankton Police Department and found them something to eat. Then he asked the dispatcher to contact the Roanoke Police Department for him. He talked to Sergeant George Wise and told him the story and about his suspicions.

Wise told him that he knew the kids. He had been to the Bailey house the week before looking for Paul Henson Jr. because he was reported as a runaway. He had seen Jennifer and her mother, Susan, arguing about the boy. The girl had her bag packed, apparently about to run away with the boy, and Paul's bag had been in the house too. It looked like he might've been living there part of the time without the mom knowing. Just about anything could have happened in that household, Wise told Kolda.

The Yankton officer felt all his alarms go off. To him, this sounded about as bad as it could get.

"What do I need to do to get you into that house without a warrant?" he asked the Roanoke officer. "I will do what you tell me to do. I think Mom's dead."

Kate's Journal

Sunday, September 28, 2008, 10 A.M.

Get call from Roanoke police. They are doing another walk around the house—I told them to get in there! They are probably all dead! Haven't heard from any of them & Susan wasn't at work again today. Said we will be in touch.

13

The Discovery

In the early morning hours of Sunday, September 28, 2008, Sergeant George Wise took a telephone call from Yankton, South Dakota. Wise listened with growing concern as Officer Eric Kolda told him about some teens he believed were runaways.

Yes, Wise said. He was familiar with those teens. He had helped search the Bailey house for Paul, and he remembered finding a note from Jennifer to Paul in Paul's wallet. It was cryptic, he told the officer on the telephone, but it mentioned going to Canada. If those kids had been heading for Canada, they would have likely gone through Oklahoma, Kansas and Nebraska and would have crossed the Nebraska–South Dakota state line at the very place where they had been stopped.

Kolda told the Texas sergeant that Jennifer Bailey claimed to be worried about her mother. She'd told him that she had tried to call her, but no one answered either her cell phone or the house telephone. Kolda also said Jennifer told him that her mother had an ex-boyfriend named "Joe" whom she'd broken up with a couple of weeks earlier, and who had since been stalking her mom "like crazy." Jennifer claimed that she was afraid of the man, and that was one reason she was going to her grandmother's house in Minnesota. "Joe" might have hurt her mother, Jennifer said.

Wise didn't especially believe that story. He suspected another culprit behind why Susan Bailey might not be answering her telephone at work or at home. Thinking back to the day he was in that house with the other officers searching for the boy and listening to the mother and daughter argue, Wise was just as suspicious as Kolda was.

Wise asked Kolda to hold the teens while he did some investigating. He'd get back to him, he said.

Meanwhile, Kolda talked to Jennifer, Paul and David again. He told them that he was holding them on a curfew charge and because Paul had been listed as a runaway. He listened to their answers to his questions. He watched them. He formed some opinions—none very good.

They said they were headed to Jennifer and David's grandparents, whose home in Minnesota lay about three hundred miles from Yankton, though Kolda surmised that they were more likely heading for Canada. The Canadian border lay about five hundred miles from Yankton. He thought they were looking for money, however, which might have been why they wanted to see the grandparents. But if they had reached the grandparents and were refused money, would they have killed them too, as he suspected they'd killed Susan Bailey? He thought they might have. He thought that was exactly what they would have done.

Kolda didn't like these kids.

The Yankton officers put the teens into separate holding cells and didn't ask any more questions. In the end, if Kolda was right, this was not going to be their case and they didn't want to do anything to mess it up.

After a while, the Yankton communications officer heard from Roanoke:

Tell your officers to hang on to those kids and to be careful, came the voice on the telephone. *We may have a ten-fifty* (code for homicide).

Sergeant Wise and several other officers drove to the house in the neighborhood of The Parks at Roanoke. They quietly pulled up in front of the two-story house on Oxford Drive at about four A.M. on Sunday, September 28, 2008, and no one stirred.

The house remained as it had been for several days. There were no lights inside, but the lights over the garage were still on. There was no car in the driveway and no apparent movement inside the house. Sergeant Wise made the decision: it was time to go inside. There was now enough probable cause that would hold up in court for checking the inside of the house without a warrant. The officers circled the big house looking for a way in without breaking anything. They found an unlocked window toward the back. Officer Moody climbed in the window and then walked to the kitchen door and unlocked it for the others.

Immediately upon entering, an unpleasant odor led

officers to believe there was something bad, very bad, waiting for them somewhere in the house.

Weapons out, they searched all the rooms on the first floor. The rooms were cluttered, but nothing appeared suspicious. Not much was different from the last time Sergeant Wise had been in the house on Tuesday, September 23. He even saw the pudding box still on the table. Then the officers climbed the stairs to the second floor.

As they reached the top of the stairs, they saw the body of a woman lying facedown on the hallway floor. There was blood on her head and shirt, and on the carpet. The back of her head was bloodied, and they thought she must have been hit with a blunt instrument. Officer Moody carefully walked around the body, then checked every room for the safety of the officers. He turned on all the lights in the eerie quiet of the empty house. Empty, save for the body of the woman facedown just to the left of the landing. No one else was there. And they knew where the other members of the household were—in custody, thank goodness.

In the bathroom of the master bedroom, Moody noted a big pile of cut brown hair and a pair of scissors lying on a blue towel on a wicker hamper. An orange extension cord hung over the shower rod. Part of it dangled near the tub. That part had been cut and the rubber had been peeled back so the wire could be frayed apart. The other end was wrapped around a doorknob and hanging near an electrical outlet. The tub was partly filled with water. Under the water he saw a big kitchen knife with a bent tip. The sight made his blood run cold. Also in the water he counted three cellular telephones. There was a rusty ring on the sides of the tub where the water had evaporated. He suspected that it was blood.

Moody reported back to his sergeant, who was standing with the others near the body. Then all the officers silently went back down the stairs, careful not to step in blood or touch anything. Sergeant Wise told a dispatcher by radio to notify all the supervisors and the detective on call. And he told them to call the Yankton officer. *Tell him*, Wise ordered, *that someone would be calling shortly with further information.*

"You tell me what you want done with them," the South Dakota officer said about the teenagers in his custody when he got the call from Texas. "I'll do anything you need."

Wise wanted photographs of the kids. *Did one of them have a fresh haircut?* he wanted to know. Kolda told him that yes, the older boy, Paul, had a hacked-off cut that looked like he had just grabbed his hair without looking and applied scissors. *Could Kolda e-mail Wise multi-angle photos of Paul's head?* Kolda said he would do it, but it would take a little while, since he'd have to drive to his own home to use his computer. (In Yankton in 2008, officers were not allowed to use a computer while at the police department. It was policy no matter the circumstances.) Kolda spent the rest of the night driving back and forth to his house, relaying information that the Roanoke officers needed.

Kolda needed more documentation to hold the teens, however, since he couldn't keep them very long on a curfew violation. He asked the sergeant to prepare arrest warrants to be served on them as soon as possible. Wise told him that it would be done.

Wise left two officers outside the front and back doors to guard the integrity of the Bailey house and drove back to the police department to begin the labor-intensive job of opening a murder investigation.

Kolda was supposed to leave his shift at seven A.M. but there was too much to be done, so he wasn't able to leave for several more hours. At eleven A.M., he drove home and went immediately to bed. But the officer was also a member of the local SWAT team—the elite Special Weapons and Tactics unit that responds to unusual, more serious situations with specialized equipment—and just an hour later he received a SWAT callout. A mentally challenged man had taken a shotgun and shot another person. The SWAT team responded and talked the man out of the house and into custody. That same afternoon, Kolda had a court appearance to testify on another case. He was running on cruise control now, fueled by adrenaline but running on "E" for exhaustion.

But no matter what, he couldn't forget those kids. They'd killed their own mother. Kolda thought about how frightened Susan Bailey must have been—how much pain she must have been in before she died. He thought about what it must have been like for the mother, seeing her children with murder in their eyes. She had given birth to them. She had bathed them and fed them and provided for their needs. And those cold-eyed children had stabbed her to death while she begged them to stop.

It had been a brutal crime. Yet the teens were so nonchalant. They'd just grabbed the dog and drove off in her car. He thought of Jennifer's glib answers to his questions and her innocent act. He had never seen anyone show such little regard for human life. Never before had he seen any-body absolutely empty inside. But those kids—all three of them—seemed truly empty.

This was pure evil, he thought. "Evil" was not even a bad enough word, but he could think of none that described fully enough what they had done.

Just before Kolda was finally able to go to sleep, he said a prayer for Susan Bailey.

Kate's Journal

Sunday, September 28, 2008 4:30 P.M.

Get call from coroner in Fort Worth. Sorry to say Susan is dead. Were they in a car accident? No—no car accident. Then how—you are going to tell me something really bad, aren't you?

14

Asking for Assistance

Roanoke Detective Brian Peterson got a call from Dispatch (the communications office) about four A.M. He was the detective on call, which traditionally meant he would be lead detective in whatever case arose on his shift. He talked to Sergeant Wise and learned what had been found inside the house on Oxford Drive.

Peterson was the son of a Texas Ranger, and had grown up in the company of his father's friends and heard their stories. Brian Peterson knew police work his whole life, and he understood the legend and the reality of the star lawmen of the Lone Star State. But he didn't start out as a law enforcement officer. Instead, he went into banking, where he worked for ten years. The lure of law enforcement was too strong, however, and in 1996 Peterson earned a peace officer's license and went to work for the Johnson County Sheriff's Office in Texas. He had stayed there for eight years and had risen to the rank of lieutenant when he moved to Roanoke in Denton County as a detective. Peterson was affable and friendly, easy to talk to and disarming. He was of medium height, with dark hair and eyes. He was handsome but he had put on a few pounds in recent years and was always trying to lose them. He had aspirations to be a sheriff one day, and he wanted to look fit when he ran for the office.

Peterson remembered his wife's prophetic caution not to jinx their lovely weekend. He recalled his talks with Susan Bailey back in 2006. She had not liked the fact that he was investigating her family, but she'd still been nice to him and helpful. She had it tough, but she was handling life with courage, he had thought. Peterson's mind drifted as he sped along the highway between his house and the Bailey home. He remembered the last time he had seen Jennifer Bailey. It was at a costume party. She was dressed as a princess. How ironic, he thought. She sure didn't seem like a princess to him now.

And David? David was just a kid. Was he really involved in this bloody mess?

Peterson was upset about Susan. He remembered sitting across the kitchen table from her and listening to her talk about Richard and her children. She was an unhappy woman but she was forthright and plainspoken. He had liked her. He knew from the start that Susan never would have allowed the kids to take her car. Now, he knew that she was dead. She had been stabbed, from the appearance of the crime scene. It looked like her children had done it. *Damn*. He dreaded seeing Susan in that condition. But it was his job to investigate, and he would do his job.

Amazingly, the Roanoke Police Department had never before had to investigate a murder. There had been accidental deaths, vehicle fatalities. But never in its entire history had an intentional killing been recorded. And now this one—matricide. A mother killed by her children. Lord, what a mess. Peterson believed he was likely to be in over his head. He wanted to handle the case right, and he needed help. He knew from the start that this case would not have a good outcome. This was just not a normal homicide, and he wanted expert advice. He considered his options, and decided it was time to call in the Texas Rangers.

The Texas Rangers are so-called because, back when they began in the early 1880s, they'd ridden horseback, ranging all over the state keeping an unruly populace at bay. That had changed. Now, one of the main tasks of the Texas Rangers, who are the most elite and highly trained law enforcement officers in the state, is to offer their experience and expertise to smaller agencies when difficult cases present themselves. Peterson knew that Ranger Tracy Murphree was assigned to work Denton County and was glad to help smaller agencies with his training and the resources of the state agency that were beyond a small town's budget. The Roanoke Police Department also had a good relationship with the Denton County Sheriff's Office, so Peterson called Sheriff's Detective Larry Kish, who called the Ranger. Both Kish and Murphree agreed to meet Peterson at the Roanoke Police Department.

Crime-scene investigator Jeff Coats was also brought on board. He was a member of the investigative bureau at the sheriff's office, but his focus was collecting and processing evidence. Coats and Roanoke Officer Shane Norman would photograph the crime scene and help Kish and other Roanoke officers with collecting evidence. When Norman had called Coats and asked for his help processing the crime scene, Coats called his sergeant and asked for permission to help the other agency. His sergeant told him that he did not have to go, since Kish was on call that weekend. But Coats believed he could be of help and volunteered to go. *OK, then*, he was told. *If that's what you want to do*. It was.

Peterson was relieved. This investigation was going to be done right. He knew he had the best help that could be found. Murphree had worked more than a hundred and fifty murder cases by the time he was asked to help out with the Roanoke stabbing. There wasn't much he had not seen, nor many criminals he had not learned to deal with. Like most Rangers, Murphree had begun as a Texas Highway Patrol officer, then worked his way up through the highway patrol ranks to specialized operations such as auto theft or narcotics investigations. The Ranger creed is "No man in the wrong can stand up against a fellow that's in the right and keeps on a-comin'."

Only the best of the best officers in the Texas Department of Public Safety ever attain the coveted rank of Ranger. In Texas, the Rangers, the oldest group of law enforcement officers on the North American continent, are legend, and among the Rangers, Murphree was widely respected.

Sheriff's Detective Larry Kish was thirty-eight in 2008. He had started his law enforcement career in Gainesville as a communications officer, or dispatcher, at eighteen years old. He left for a few years while he attended Sam Houston State University near Houston, Texas, then was hired in Denton as a communications officer and later became a patrol officer there. He moved to the Denton County Sheriff's Office in 1995. He and Jeff Coats were around the same age and had worked as crime-scene techs in 2008, but Kish later became a detective and then a detective sergeant, and Coats's official title was Forensic Investigator Tech II.

Peterson was glad to have Kish, Murphree and Coats on board to help. They were quality officers. He could learn from them.

Once at the police department, Peterson, Kish and Murphree conferred. They didn't want to go in without a warrant. The officers knew what lay inside the house and they knew they were looking at a capital murder case. They wanted every "t" crossed and every "i" dotted.

In Texas, capital murder is a death penalty case. If the kids had murdered Susan, and if they did it in the course of committing another felony, such as stealing her car or credit cards, that would qualify as a capital case. An alternative to the death penalty would be life in prison without parole. These were teenagers, but the officers knew what lay at the top of the stairs in the house. If everything was as it appeared right then, they qualified for a charge of first-degree murder.

That Sunday afternoon, Murphree wrote an affidavit with Peterson's help, and then Jeff Coats took it to District Judge Bruce McFarling at his home in Denton. McFarling, a former Denton County prosecutor, could always be counted on to read affidavits whatever time of the day or night law enforcement officers needed a warrant. He also was known as a fair judge whose decisions on the bench were not overturned. He was respected by both prosecutors and defense lawyers. McFarling was meticulous.

Kish waited with Murphree, who was his good friend, until the search warrant arrived. While they were waiting, Murphree made a telephone call to Victoria Abbott, who was chief of the juvenile division of the Denton County District Attorney's Office. Murphree told her they had what they believed was going to be a capital murder case involving at least two juveniles. (Jennifer's eighteenth birthday was less than a week away, and under Texas law, she became a legal adult at seventeen.) He wanted to make sure that everything was done exactly right, he told her. He was seeking advice. Abbott listened to the story as they knew it so far and told Murphree what needed to happen to preserve the legal rights of the juveniles. Prosecuting anyone under the age of seventeen was completely different from prosecuting an adult defendant. It was a bit tricky, and Abbott told him everything she could think of that would keep the officers out of legal trouble. These were kids who did not need to get off on a technicality, she thought.

The Denton County officers were impressed by the activities going on at the Roanoke Police Department on a Sunday, when few officers were supposed to be on duty. The entire command staff was there, including the police chief. Everyone had a task and was carrying it out. The chief told the Ranger and Kish and Coats that whatever they needed, they would have. He arranged for them to carry access badges, which allowed them access into the locked parts of the building. He told them that each of them would have a telephone and computer in the war room he was setting up in his training room, which would be designated off-limits to anyone not working on the case.

The other officers were still working at myriad tasks, and the four main investigators talked over what they knew so far. Then they all drove to the house on Oxford Drive. They canvassed the neighborhood, talking to neighbors to find out if anyone had seen anything unusual at the house, or if anyone knew the family. Most neighbors said that the Baileys were quiet and kept mostly to themselves, but one neighbor told them about a recent event where David had been outdoors naked. The neighbor swore he'd seen the boy masturbating to the rhythm of a water sprinkler that traveled around the yard. The police had been called, but by then David had gone back inside the house, the neighbor said. Another neighbor had heard a rumor that David had killed the family cat down in the park, but the officers couldn't confirm that. They never did find the cat, however.

The Parks of Roanoke was a really nice neighborhood of big, mostly two-story houses in the half-million-dollar range. It was not the kind of neighborhood where they usually worked murder cases, the investigators thought. It was a neighborhood any one of them would like to live in. Coats described the scene in a report. The front of the house faced north, he wrote. They entered facing south, toward the back of the house. On the left, just inside the front door, was a door to the garage. The first room they entered was a formal living room, which contained a small amount of furniture and a bare Christmas tree. It was late September, and Coats thought it was odd to see the decoration at that time of year. He saw a small powder room on the west side of that room. Next, heading south, there was a formal dining room full of furniture, decorations and a lot of clutter. Coats noted the air-conditioning control panel was in this room and it was set on eighty degrees. Behind the dining room was the eat-in kitchen, which contained another dining table near the south wall of the house. There was a back door in that wall, and it led to a big backyard with a picnic table, a grill and a small storage shed. A family room was the final first-floor room, and the stairway to the second floor began on the left side of the family room.

Coats wrote in his report that a small area with a window lay at the top of the stairway. To the right was a large, very cluttered game room. To access the bedrooms, it was necessary to turn left down a hallway. Susan Bailey's body lay prone on the landing nearly in front of the first doorway on the hall. That appeared to be a girl's bedroom. Continuing south now, the next door led to a second bedroom that appeared to be used as an office and storage space. Next to it was a third bedroom with bunk beds and items a boy might have in his room. Next to that was a hall bathroom and, rounding a corner, the door to the master bedroom. Inside that bedroom was a second upstairs bathroom. Next to the fourth bedroom, Coats, having finished a circuit of hallways on the second floor that surrounded the opening for the staircase, came again to the game room.

Coats wrote in his report that he went back down the stairs and out the front door to the porch, where the other officers waited. Then they began their investigation. They looked carefully at the front and back doors and at all the windows in the house. There was no sign of forced entry. No stranger had broken into the house to do this deed.

Detective Peterson began an audio recording as the rest of the officers walked through the front door. He described the scene as they looked briefly through the downstairs and then climbed to the second-floor hallway. Murphree also described the scene in his report, noting a white female lying facedown on the carpet dressed in jeans, a bloody blue shirt and white socks. What the original officers had thought might be a wound from a blunt object turned out to be numerous stab wounds in the back of the woman's head, the report stated. Murphree noted that her throat had been cut. The wound gaped open. He noted blood on the wall and a bedroom door with bloodstains consistent with an arterial spray. The blood was low on the wall, indicating she had already been down—perhaps on her knees—when her throat and that artery had been cut.

When an artery, such as the carotid in the neck, has been cut, blood that is being pumped from the heart spurts out with each heartbeat. There were not many of the blood spray marks meaning she had not lived long after she was down. Her heart had quickly stopped forcing out blood.

Murphree also noted that there was a blood smear on the carpet that appeared to have been transferred from a hand and fingers being wiped on the carpet.

Someone wiped the blood off their hands right there beside her.

Drying blood is sticky and smells coppery. Most of this blood had dried already, but there was so much of it that the carpet underneath the body still looked wet.

The officers found two bandanas on the carpet near the body, both tied in the classic elongated triangle of a robber's mask. They had earlier noticed a third bandana downstairs. Robbers' masks? Really? Had those kids really thought that their mother wouldn't recognize them with kerchiefs across the lower portions of their faces? Or were they supposed to make police believe that strangers had done this evil deed? The crime in its totality was a combination of brutal violence and childish fantasy. Jennifer, David and Paul were murderers, but they were also children. *We'll attack our mother with knives while wearing bandanas like Old West robbers, and she won't know who's stabbing her before she dies.* Right. Just like in the old western movies on TV.

"These kids were evil," Kish said later. "It's not like they had a bad upbringing."

The officers entered the master bedroom and bath and saw the piles of hair on the wicker basket and the vanity and the pair of scissors on the blue towel beside the hair. Somebody wanted to change his or her appearance, they deduced. They noted the bright orange extension cord over the tub and the knife and three cellular telephones under about a foot of water. The water had a faint blue tint and a slight chemical odor, and they believed that some sort of cleaner had been added to the tub. Coats asked for clean new plastic buckets to collect the knife and cell phones from the bathtub. Peterson called his chief, who sent an officer to Home Depot to buy the buckets and deliver them to the crime scene. Then Coats collected the phones and the knife by placing the five-gallon buckets, one at a time, into the tub and under the water. He ran each bucket along the bottom, collecting water along with each phone and the knife. He then placed lids on the buckets and sealed the evidence into the buckets with the water they were found in. The crime-scene officers placed the towel, scissors and hair in separate evidence bags. For some reason, that pile of hacked-off hair was disturbing, even more unsettling than it perhaps should have been, given the blood and the body the investigators had to step over to proceed with their investigation.

They noted in their reports that nothing appeared to have been stolen and there were no signs of forced entry.

They found a bowl full of a foul-smelling, lumpy, moldy substance and realized it was the nasty chocolate pudding that Susan had refused to eat. No one had bothered to throw it away. They found the instant pudding box that it came from, and they took both into evidence. They had read about the pudding incident when they went over the prior Roanoke police reports generated from the house. The pudding would be tested to determine whether it contained some kind of poison.

They found on the dining room table a receipt from the nearby Walmart store dated Thursday, September 25. The receipt was for some kind of game cards and a bottle of Formula 409 cleaner. They found the half-empty cleaner bottle on a picnic table on the back patio slab. Peterson relayed the information to another Roanoke officer, who went to the nearby Walmart and obtained a surveillance video for the time the cleaner was purchased. The video showed David Bailey riding up on his bicycle, entering the store, finding the cleaner and going through the self-checkout lane to pay for it. He placed the cleaner and the game cards in his backpack and rode away.

This showed planning. They'd bought the cleaner before Susan came home. So much for David being an innocent bystander. The cleaner had been sprayed on the cell phones and the knife before they were thrown in the water in the master bathtub, the detectives believed. And they could smell it on Susan's body. The detectives thought the kids had believed they could eliminate fingerprints or maybe DNA that way.

The master bedroom had a big king-size bed and formal red-and-gold curtains. The bed had shelves and drawers that extended its width along one wall. The bedspread matched the curtains and the bed skirt was made in the same stripes as the pullbacks on the curtains. So much care had been taken in the decorating of a house where such a terrible crime had taken place.

Inside a drawer in Susan's bedroom, investigators discovered a single one-hundred-dollar bill. In another drawer, they found a ten. If the kids had found this cash, they likely wouldn't have run out of money and wouldn't have been trying to steal gasoline when Officer Kolda found them. It's possible that they would have made it to Canada.

The officers found a homemade bat on the bed they had determined was in Jennifer's room. It looked as though those kids had set up a murder house, with weapons at every turn. In Jennifer's bedroom, the officers also found a coiled metal ring with two identification cards attached. They were Northwest High School IDs for Paul Henson and Merrilee White. They looked inside a black handbag in the room and discovered more items that also belonged to Merrilee. Who was this Merrilee White?

They needed to find her, Murphree told Peterson. Merrilee was probably involved in all of this. Peterson contacted his office, and he soon reported back that Merrilee White was a fourteen-year-old girl who had been in juvenile detention in Fort Worth since Tuesday morning after trying to attack her mother with a butcher knife. So, Murphree said, she could not have been involved in the stabbing of Susan Bailey because she was in police custody when it occurred, but it appeared highly likely that Merrilee had somehow been involved in this murder conspiracy.

Fort Worth police had another message about Merrilee White. When they had asked her about Paul Henson, she'd told them that he was her boyfriend. And when they'd asked her about a gun, she'd said, "If he has a gun, then the plan is in motion."

It was obvious now that there had been some sort of plan involving at least these four teens. There had been a conspiracy to murder. The officers were shocked. The youngest of these kids was thirteen years old.

The officers took a number of things from the house as evidence. They took anything that might have been used as a weapon, including a box cutter and numerous knives and forks both from the dirty dishes in the kitchen and the clean dishes in the dishwasher. They seized the half-empty bottle of Formula 409 cleaner and the receipt from Walmart that showed when it had been purchased. They bagged up the school identification cards for Jennifer, Paul and Merrilee. They found Jennifer's wallet and Susan's wallet and took them along as evidence. They collected a notepad with seven pages of written notes and a spiral notebook from Jennifer's room. They took computers from the house, as well as Jennifer's entire bedroom door. They found two pairs of scissors and a hammer in the bedrooms upstairs. They picked up all three bandanas, placing them into separate evidence bags, hoping to find DNA on them. They took numerous swabs of bloodstains and splashes throughout the hallway area and a cutting from a bloodstain on Jennifer's bed. They took the hair, presumed to be Paul's, and the evil-looking extension cord with its frayed end. They found a possible fingerprint in blood on a bathroom tile and cut out the whole tile. They also took the shower curtain. They picked up a clean Band-Aid from the driveway and took empty Band-Aid wrappers from the downstairs bathroom and the living room. They took two samples of the noxious pudding and the package it was made from.

Meanwhile, Roanoke police were still working on arrest warrants for Jennifer, Paul and David. The charge was capital murder. After the judge signed the warrants, they were forwarded to Yankton police and served on the three teens, and they were moved to a juvenile detention facility in Sioux Falls, South Dakota.

Officer Kolda took pictures of each teen before they were taken away and collected all their clothing as evidence. Then he e-mailed the photos to Roanoke. Murphree noted in his report that the pile of hair on the wicker basket was the same color as Paul's and that in his photo he now sported a crudely hacked-off haircut. Someone referred to him as "the bad haircut boy."

Kolda had done an amazing job, the detectives decided. Without his help they would not be so far along in this case.

15

The Medical Examiner Investigation

Denton County contracts with the Tarrant County Medical Examiner's Office for autopsies, and Tarrant County in turn contracts with a private physician whose company provides doctors for the forensic work. The system is a bit clumsy, but it works. Denton County has its own death investigators who respond to the scenes of remains found under suspicious circumstances or of any person who dies alone. The Denton County investigators work with the Tarrant County Medical Examiner's Office. They investigate at the scene and bring their results to the doctors, who perform the autopsies. Unlike on TV, doctors in Texas don't respond to the scene themselves but use their investigators as their eyes and ears. The bodies are transported to Fort Worth by funeral-home van. The funeral home also is under contract to Denton County to provide the service.

Death Investigator Sharon Baughman entered the house

at The Parks of Roanoke and climbed the stairs to begin her duties. She noted that it was 1:38 P.M., Sunday, September 28 when the search warrant arrived and everyone went inside the house. The air was heavy with portent and the smell of death.

Baughman was an experienced investigator. She began a career in law enforcement with the Denton police in 1984. When Denton County opened an office for death investigators in 1989, she applied and was hired. In 2008, Baughman was working weekends. Several investigators shared duties on a rotating basis, but none of them liked to work weekends except Baughman, who had sought out the shift. She preferred how she could respond from home as fast as from the office in Denton, and after her weekend stint she then had most of the rest of the week off. Tarrant County Medical Examiner Nizam Peerwani liked to hire former law enforcement officers as investigators. But Baughman knew that Peerwani preferred that his investigators not have current law enforcement licenses. Sworn officers were obligated to read a suspect his Miranda rights before questioning him. The unsworn medical examiner investigators did not, so they could get the first, unrehearsed story that could then be compared to the story a suspect told after being advised of his rights by a police officer. The investigators interviewed anyone who had been at the scene at the time of death or who had made the discovery. These were experienced interviewers and they knew the questions to ask. But they did not operate under the same legal obligations as sworn law enforcement officers. In this case, no one alive remained in the Bailey house for Baughman to interview.

Baughman had a standard way of approaching a crime

scene. First she went straight to the body to get an idea of what she was working with. She hadn't been told anything in advance about what she would find in the house at The Parks of Roanoke except that there was a deceased person there. Baughman preferred it that way. It prevented her from approaching a scene with a preconceived notion of what had happened. If, for instance, she had been told there was a reported suicide at a location, she would arrive with the idea that she was working on a case where someone had killed themselves, which might cause her to miss clues that the case was not a suicide at all. She wanted a clean slate to begin with. She wanted to make her own decisions.

Once Baughman climbed the stairs at the Bailey house and looked at the body, she noted there was a strong odor of some kind of cleaner on Susan. Baughman went back outside. She photographed the street sign. Oxford Drive, it said. She photographed the street number on the house and the yard. *Odd that something like this could happen in such a nice house in such an upper-middle-class neighborhood*, she thought, just as the other investigators had. Baughman worked her way in, looking at everything in the house and photographing everything for the record. Her photo files would give the doctors a full view of the surroundings where the remains they were working on had been found.

Before the officers began bagging the evidence, Baughman photographed it so she could present a clear picture of the crime scene to the medical examiner. She photographed the dining table that held the receipt from Walmart for the cleaner. She noted that the time stamp was for 5:35 P.M. on Thursday. She knew that the victim had last been seen alive at about eleven thirty P.M. on Thursday. *Someone knew they were going to have a mess to clean up long before Susan Bailey was stabbed*, she realized. Not that someone had done a good job of that, she thought. But the time stamp on the purchase clearly indicated intent. And prior intent is important in a murder case.

She noticed again the strong odor of cleaning solution around the body. Maybe the kids thought they could wash off fingerprints or DNA that way. Forensic television shows made people think they knew all about murder and how to avoid getting caught. The tub where someone had thrown three cell phones and a big knife with a bent tip also smelled of the same cleaning solution she had noted on the body. There were deep finger indentions in a bar of soap. Someone had clenched it tightly while showering.

Baughman worked closely with law enforcement officers at crime scenes. She made it a point not to disturb anything until they were ready for her to begin. Susan Bailey was lying facedown on the hallway floor. At some point, the body would have to be turned faceup. She first photographed the body as it lay, then she and some of the officers turned over the body and Baughman began making photographs and taking notes.

Sheriff's Detective Larry Kish was one of the officers who helped turn Susan's heavy, inert body. It was difficult. The term "dead weight" is apropos. The deceased can offer no help in moving his or her heavy center mass and loose appendages. When the investigators turned Susan's body faceup, they accidentally compressed the abdomen as they maneuvered, and blood squirted from some of the wounds. The expelled blood hit Kish in the face, head, right arm and right leg. Decidedly unpleasant. But also potentially dangerous. There is a process for documenting the exposure of an officer to blood. Kish carefully washed the blood away, making sure he didn't miss any. He called his wife to bring him fresh clothing. He filled out a report explaining how he happened to come into contact with blood. Later, he went to a medical facility and had blood drawn for routine tests. He had not been contaminated with anything, but it was policy to make sure.

Baughman reported that the body was cool to the touch and very little rigor remained, although Susan's hands still were clenched in rigor mortis. "Rigor mortis" is Latin for "stiffness in death." Rigor begins at the time of death and usually is noticeable two to four hours after death. The body gets stiffer and stiffer and rigor generally is complete eighteen to twenty-four hours after death. The stiffness generally will begin to relax somewhere between thirty-six to forty-eight hours after death. In Susan's body, rigor mortis was almost over. Most of the body had lost the stiffness, and the stiffness was easily broken in the parts that still showed signs of the effect. Carefully, with her gloved hands, Baughman straightened Susan's fingers.

Liver mortis, or lividity, is usually fixed between eighteen and twenty-four hours after death and does not go away. The pooling of blood caused by gravity that is called liver mortis tends to allow the blood to settle in the parts of the body closest to the floor. Blood had pooled in Susan's face and stomach, and it looked certain that she had not been moved from the place where she had died. There was a contusion to the left eye, as though she had been struck. Perhaps that had been the work of the baseball bat. Baughman noted the blood-sodden carpet under the body and the strong smells competing with the odor of bleach. The olfactory sense is the strongest one a person possesses. Bad smells start emanating from a body a few hours after death. In this case, it was about sixty hours after death; working closely with the remains was not pleasant.

In movies, TV shows and books about medical examiners, much is made about the time of death. Fictional investigators use thermometers to determine core body heat and compare it with ambient temperature of the place of death. It's possible that MEs in some parts of the United States do this, but not in North Texas. The Tarrant County Medical Examiner does not believe that comparing body temperature with ambient temperature is a scientific way of discerning time of death. In fact, the medical examiner does not recognize any scientific way to decide on a time of death. There are too many variables, he believes. So while Baughman noted that the thermostat remained at eighty degrees that hot September day in Texas, she made no assumptions from that about the time Susan had died. Instead, investigators worked from Susan's last known movements. Since she'd left Hurst at 11:30 P.M., she would have arrived at her home about midnight, and she hadn't shown up for work the next morning. That narrowed down the time of death; however, as per standard procedure, her time of death was officially listed as the time when the body first was found by the Roanoke officers.

Baughman brought out a clean white sheet, and the officers helped her roll Susan's body onto it and wrap the sheet tightly.

Any trace evidence that had been left on or under the body would go to the morgue with the body for examination.

Baughman thought of the nasty pudding she had seen in a bowl in Susan's bathroom and the larger bowl downstairs. She noted the butcher knife found under Jennifer's bed and the baseball bat lying on top of it. There had been a gun somewhere in the house, she learned. And the frayed electrical cord hung ready for a possible electrocution. The officers she was working with believed this woman's children killed her. Baughman was amazed and horrified at the number of ways those kids had thought of to do their mother in.

When Baughman was finished with Susan, she called Susan's mother, Kate Morten. That was part of her duty as a death investigator. It was not a pleasant job, and she usually had to notify next of kin in person. But Minnesota was a long way from Roanoke, Texas. And Susan's mother already suspected that something was wrong. She wanted answers sooner rather than later, and Baughman thought Kate would rather hear the truth from someone who was at the scene than a local Minnesota officer, dispatched to deliver the tragic announcement, who would have no real information for her.

So Baughman called Kate and told her that her daughter was dead. *How?* Kate wanted to know. Had there been a traffic accident? No, Baughman told her as gently as she could. Susan had been stabbed multiple times. She had been found in the upstairs hallway of her house. And her children had been found in South Dakota in Susan's car. They were suspects in her death.

What a tragedy, Sharon Baughman thought. *How could a mother and grandmother endure such a thing?*

Kate's Journal

Sunday, September 28, 2008, 4:30 P.M.

In shock—knew it!

Can't find Stephen!!! Hollering!!! Ears [hearing aids] out and he can't hear—there he is on the dock working on the boat. I'm hollering he's not coming! Finally I tell him they found Susan & she's dead. We are crying. Neighbor comes running over and says what's the matter. Must think we are hurt. Yell at him our daughter was found murdered and the kids did it!

16

The Trip to South Dakota

On Monday, September 29, 2008, Texas Ranger Tracy Murphree arranged with the agency he worked for, the Texas Department of Public Safety, for the use of the agency's small airplane to transport himself, Sheriff's Detective Larry Kish and Roanoke Detective Brian Peterson to Sioux Falls, South Dakota. Once they landed, they rented a car and drove to the Minnehaha County Regional Juvenile Detention Center, where their young suspects—Jennifer and David Bailey and Paul Henson Jr.—had all been taken. There they attempted to interview Jennifer, who at nearly eighteen was the only one who was legally an adult. But she sat stubbornly silent and would not look at the investigators, let alone answer their questions. She was cold and unemotional. The only thing Murphree got out of her was the answer to one question: *Why did you kill your mother?*

Her answer: "We just didn't see eye to eye."

Internally, Murphree shuddered at the cold response. But he had seen too much death and too many killers to show any exterior emotion now.

"Jennifer," Murphree said instead, "this is your first murder. But it's not mine."

The officers noticed that the girl's knuckles were red and swollen. There were small nicks and cuts on her hands, and when they asked a female officer to pull down her shirt, they could see scratches on her back and shoulders. They carefully used measuring tools to document each injury and took photos. The pictures would show that Jennifer had been in a struggle with someone, someone who'd been fighting for her life against the girl.

When the investigators attempted to speak to Paul, he seemed to be in some sort of trance. He was there, and yet he was not there. His eyes were vacant. *The boy was weird*, they thought. Paul had a strange wound on his left arm. It was long and shallow and very red. It ran across the front of his forearm about halfway between his shoulder and elbow. When Murphree asked him about it, Paul said, oh, he did that himself, just cut it a little and sucked on it. Paul was a cutter, the officers realized. It obviously had been cut and sucked over and over. Kish photographed that too.

They did not attempt to further interview the boys because of their juvenile status. They would wait until they got back to Texas, and they would make sure it was done just right.

They left the suspects there for the time being, and then they drove to Yankton and met Officer Eric Kolda, without whose diligence they would not have these three capital murder suspects in custody. If not for his investigation on a routine traffic stop, the teens would be in Canada by then. They may or may not ever have been found and returned to the United States. The sharp policeman had saved them days of searching for the runaways and untold problems getting them extradited to the United States.

Kolda had a couple more pieces of information for them. An officer who was overseeing Paul had heard him making a telephone call to his father. On the call, Paul had denied any involvement whatsoever in the stabbing of Susan Bailey. *David did it*, he'd told his dad. He also had told one of the other officers that he wasn't involved in the murder.

The investigators from Texas also met with Gretchen Slate of the South Dakota State Attorney General's Office to prepare an affidavit for searching the blue Saturn, currently secured in a warehouse in Yankton. After a circuit judge signed the warrant, they made their way to the warehouse and processed the blue 2002 four-door automobile.

They found one of Susan's credit cards in the car and several receipts that showed apparent failed attempts to use the card at various ATMs along their way. They also found a few articles of clothing. A pair of shorts and a pair of panties in the car were bloodstained. There was no luggage in the car. The teens were traveling light. The officers assumed that the teens likely panicked after Susan was dead and could not remain in the house with a corpse. They figured the kids decided it was time to leave for Canada, and they didn't take time to repack their bags. Young people often are not good planners. What they would do when they reached their destination with no clothing, no food and no money did not seem to have crossed their young minds. If it had, perhaps the sight of their own mother in a bloody heap on the floor in front of Jennifer's bedroom door had driven those thoughts away.

Kish swabbed several car surfaces for blood. He recorded and placed into evidence bags swabs from a key to the car and a spot on the fabric of the seat. He took a swab from one of the armrests and from the inside and outside door handles all the way around the car. He even swabbed the brake and gas pedals and took swabs from the steering wheel, the gear shift and the dashboard. He also took all the miscellaneous clothing into evidence as well as "death cards" from some sort of card game. He photographed everything.

There were very few articles of real evidentiary value. The officers had still not found the missing Ruger pistol. After securing the car back in the storage compartment, they said good-bye to Officer Kolda, and the three Texas officers drove back to the airport. Then they boarded the DPS plane for a return flight. There was a lot of work waiting for them in Texas.

Murphree later referred to that Monday as "that week we spent in South Dakota one day."

Susan's ex-husband, Richard Bailey, notified Yankton police that he would be picking up the car in the next few days. Asked about Ginger, he indicated he did not want the dog, and he signed a release giving up ownership. Ginger would remain in the animal shelter until the unlikely event that she was adopted, or until she was destroyed. Ginger lost her home, her family and most likely her life. She was another victim of the crime at the house in The Parks of Roanoke.

17

The Autopsy

The autopsy of Susan Bailey was performed that same Monday, September 29, 2008, while the other officers were in South Dakota. Crime-scene investigator Jeff Coats and some Roanoke officers attended. Coats videotaped the autopsy. When the body was opened with the standard "Y" cut, the smell of old blood permeated the room. Autopsies are never pleasant to watch. But because of the length of time between death and the discovery of the body, this one was worse than most. The pathologist pointed out various wounds. Many of them could have been the fatal wound, and there was no way to tell which one had been the killing cut. One wound penetrated the spine and severed the larynx.

Susan's throat had been cut twice. Another wound showed that a large knife had penetrated the lower left side of her back and penetrated into the abdomen. The official autopsy report stated the cause of death was "multiple stab and incised wounds of the neck due to assault by another person." The manner of death was ruled "homicide," which simply means, "death at the hand of another person."

The report noted that the body had arrived wrapped in a white cloth inside a blue vinyl remains bag. A Bed Bath & Beyond name tag still was pinned to her blue blouse, and underneath, Susan had worn a pink bra and underwear. Pink had always been her favorite color.

The cervical spine had been fractured and the spinal cord had been cut. The larynx had been fractured and the left carotid artery and jugular vein had been cut.

Internally, time and injury had taken their toll over the days her body had lain alone in the hallway of an empty house, and most organs were decomposed. The precise, scientific language of the medical examiner's report nevertheless told a horrifying story.

With the blood washed off and the wounds clean and visible, Coats realized he was looking at the effects of pure rage. The person who was behind Susan, whom he suspected must have been Paul, had been strong and those wounds were deep and ugly. Some wounds in the front seemed to be from a different knife and were not as deep. They showed signs of hesitation in their pattern. He thought they probably were delivered by Jennifer. Some wounds on the left side were barely more than scratches. He thought they were likely David's contribution to his mother's death.

The pathologist's drawings of Susan's head and body showed nine stab wounds on the lower back of her head. The skull most likely had been a hard barrier for the big but fairly flimsy knife, which likely accounted for its bent tip. Some of these cuts severed the spinal cord. The drawings showed a cut behind the left ear and a cut behind the right ear. There were two long, deep cuts across the throat and three short, shallow cuts there. There were two cuts on the back. One, on the upper left shoulder, was shallow and appeared to have been a knife-tip cut. The second was midway on the left back. Five shallow cuts or scratches marked the upper right chest. There were defensive cuts on the left hand. The pathologist counted twenty-six separate wounds in all.

What had happened in that hallway, with a mother swarmed by her children and a strong teenage boy, was simply awful.

18

Another Visit to the House

Ranger Tracy Murphree and Investigator Larry Kish talked about the case on Wednesday, October 1, 2008. It would be a good idea, they decided, to return to the house on Oxford Drive with Leuco Crystal Violet, a chemical used to enhance bloodstains. Bloody fingerprints could be captured this way. And if Paul Henson Jr. was claiming he had nothing to do with the murder, they wanted to be sure to find all his fingerprints near the crime scene.

They notified Detective Brian Peterson and Investigator Jeff Coats, the county's crime-scene specialist. And Murphree wrote another affidavit for a search warrant for the house in The Parks of Roanoke.

This search was more leisurely and less stressful without the body present, although dark, nearly black stains still marked the place where Susan Bailey had died. The officers began at the front door, where a rosebush blooming in

Susan's favorite pale pink offset the warning of the yellow-and-black crime-scene tape. The yard was tidy but could have used a mowing by that time. It was dotted with shrubbery and a few small trees. Out back, another rosebush was in bloom. This one was in hot pink. A row of tall shrubs gave the yard privacy from the house behind it. The yard contained a small storage building and a picnic table on a concrete slab. Ashes in a barbecue pit showed evidence of happier times.

Coats made an initial walk-through, photographing everything so there would be a before-and-after comparison. Then Coats, Kish, Murphree and Peterson walked inside. The drapery looked formal and expensive, but actually, Susan had made the beautiful drapes herself. She had been an excellent seamstress. A small living room was mostly empty of furniture, but a windowlike opening showed off the dining room, and the shelflike bottom of the opening was decorated with crystal and candles. Susan had loved beautiful things. But the house had suffered while she'd worked two jobs and the kids had refused to help keep it clean. Just by the front door, a coatrack and shelf ran for a few feet. The floor beneath was littered with several pairs of shoes, and there were coats on the rack despite the warm weather outside. On the shelf, Coats photographed an odd collection of things: a big rock, an umbrella, a red dog leash, a notepad and an eleven-by-fourteen-inch photograph in a frame of Jennifer and Paul in their prom outfits.

The family room also had heavy drapes, lovely flower arrangements, cushy microfiber furniture, handsome lamps and a fireplace. They looked again at the denuded synthetic Christmas tree in the living room. Had it been put up very early or left up extremely late? The officers were betting the latter.

The dining table and chairs were heavy, beautiful and appeared to be antiques or at least good reproductions. They matched the handsome china cabinet with its load of china and crystal. It would have looked elegant, had the table not been littered with a messy assortment of items, and there was an empty pizza box on the floor.

The kitchen island contained three one-gallon milk jugs, some with soured milk inside. A big package of ramen noodles sat next to two large jars of peanuts, along with a half-eaten slice of watermelon with a big knife beside it. There seemed to be a lot of kitchen knives in this house.

Attached to the refrigerator door by a magnet they found a record of school discipline against David. He had taken a knife to school and received three days of in-school suspension.

The officers moved up the stairs, with Coats photographing family pictures stair-stepping up the wall. They looked into the game room and shook their heads. Books and compact discs had been pulled off the room-length shelves and, along with children's clothing, scattered on the floor.

They moved into Jennifer's room. Susan had painted the room a pretty blue, and the curtains and matching coverlet were in blue and spring green. Stuffed animals sat on shelves and her dresser. A pretty doll and Jennifer's graduation mortarboard lay on her closet shelf. But the room carpet was basically invisible under the piles of clothing. From one of the piles they pulled a pair of girl's size four jeans. They appeared to have blood on them. The jeans were placed in a large plastic bag along with an evidence sheet. Kish looked at the tags on the blouses and jeans. They were all expensive, brand-name items from stores where teens liked to shop, he said. Susan had worked hard to give her children things they wanted as well as things they needed. And they had repaid her with violence and death.

On Jennifer's unmade bed lay a baseball bat, part of her arsenal for murdering her mother. The stabbing had taken place right outside her bedroom door, and the officers imagined her stepping out of her room to greet her mother with a knife. They found more blood in the room when Kish sprayed the Leuco Crystal Violet (LCV). When they pulled back the covers, they found a big yellow rubber glove, obviously the mate to the one found on David's bunk bed during the first search of the house.

David's bunk beds were made up with red sheets, which looked cheerful against the yellow walls of his room. The officers had no idea what the gloves had been used for. Maybe part of their efforts to clean up the blood, they thought.

A fourth bedroom seemed to be used as an office and for storage. It was very cluttered.

Susan's bedroom was different. It was done in a dark royal red and gold. She had a wall bed, with drawers and shelves extending on either side of the sleeping area. The bed had been made but the crimson spread was in disarray, as though Jennifer and Paul might have spent some time there. Susan's walk-in closet was meticulous. Her clothing hung in two neat lines, and thought seemed to have been given to the order of dresses and pants and robes. Tidy rows of plastic storage boxes lined the upper shelves. This was the true Susan. The Susan who was too busy and too exhausted to force her children to clean up after themselves, and who suffered at the sight of her messy kitchen but was too tired to clean it up, at least managed to take pride in her organized closet, a space that was hers alone.

Kish swabbed numerous areas that had turned purple with bloodstains. He looked carefully for fingerprints and in some cases cut out sections of the wall to preserve them. If Paul was claiming that he had nothing to do with Susan's murder, then it was important to tie him to the scene by finding his fingerprints in the blood. Kish was sure the teen had been involved and he was determined to prove it. Neither David nor Jennifer was strong enough to have inflicted those deep wounds. The officers moved into the place of their primary interest. The master bathroom was a good spot to collect bloody fingerprints, and blood showed up violet when sprayed with the chemical substance. The LCV turned the room into a house of horrors. The teens had apparently tried to haphazardly wipe blood away and spray the cleaner around, but much of it showed up regardless. Splash marks up the tub glowed purple. Those kids had been bloody when they bathed. The purple glow of the blood looked obscene.

They photographed numerous fingerprints and blood smears in both bathrooms and even in the powder room downstairs. Someone had washed blood off themselves in the sink there, the LCV spray showed. In two cases they actually cut the fingerprints out of a bathroom wall. The officers believed that David probably showered in the hall bathroom while Jennifer and Paul cleaned up in Susan's tub. They figured that Jennifer had cut off Paul's mop of hair to make him less recognizable in case people began looking for them.

Blood splashes turned the tiles above the tubs purple. The bar of soap with deep impressions where it had been clutched by tense fingers indicated someone not as stoic as he or she wanted to appear. They collected the bar of soap as evidence.

In the common hall bathroom, the shower curtain was covered in purple splashes. They took it down and placed the whole curtain into evidence.

"Those kids had a lot of blood on them," Peterson said later. "I hate to think what they might have done to her. They are the spawn of Satan."

19

Search for the Truth

Roanoke Police Chief Gary Johnson had held the position since May of 2003. Before that, he had worked in the nearby town of Watauga. Johnson had thirty sworn officers on his force, and when he began organizing the mechanics of the case on that Monday, he committed several of them to help out. In addition to Detective Brian Peterson, Johnson asked the other two detectives on staff to help as needed. And he wanted Patrol Sergeant George Wise on the case. Wise had been involved since the beginning. He had seen Susan interact with her daughter. He had seen the house before she died in it. Wise was a good addition to the small task force.

In the long history of Roanoke, this was the first recorded case of murder, and it was a doozy. Not only was it vicious and bloody, it involved juveniles. The police department building was fairly new, and the city judge and courtroom also were housed there. The offices looked modern and well appointed. Chief Johnson decided to turn his big training room into a war room for the case. He first added deadbolt locks to the doors. Only officers involved in working the case would have keys. He wanted his evidence secure and the details kept quiet. He set up workstations in the room for Ranger Tracy Murphree, Sheriff's Investigator Larry Kish, Peterson and the other Roanoke officers who would be closely involved in gathering evidence. He instructed the officers to use the big dry-erase board to keep track. They were to write everything on the board. That way, any time he walked into the room he could update himself on the progress they were making instead of having to interrupt them to ask. Johnson knew that forging a capital case was difficult at best, and given the circumstances that they were dealing with here, he wanted everything done exactly right.

There did not seem to be much doubt that the teens were involved, Johnson thought. The house had been secure when officers arrived. There was no sign of forced entry, and the teens had fled in the car. But police cannot ever just assume something. There had to be proof for each allegation, so every effort was made to substantiate every clue.

On Wednesday, October 1, Johnson sent four officers (three male officers and one female officer, because they would have a female prisoner) in two squad cars to South Dakota to bring the teens, now officially capital murder suspects, back to Denton County. At first, the transport officers put Jennifer and David in one car and Paul in the other. That didn't last long. When Murphree heard this, he told Peterson to instruct the officers to move David to the car holding Paul. An adult prisoner should not ride with juvenile prisoners, Murphree said, and Jennifer was legally an adult. Peterson passed along the information and the cars stopped and switched passengers. The officers guarding Jennifer told her not to talk about the case. *Don't talk to us about your mother or taking the car or anything else about your mom and the way you left the house*, they said. So Jennifer talked about California. She had lived there before coming to Texas and she loved it. She loved the beach, she said. She didn't like Texas because it was hot. And in the summer, her mother didn't turn up the air-conditioning to save money. They had fans in their bedrooms and in the family rooms to stir the air. In the winter her mother didn't turn up the heat high enough, the girl complained. Jennifer said her bedroom was over the garage and was colder in winter and hotter in summer than some of the other rooms. It was uncomfortable, she whined. *Uncomfortable enough to warrant murder?* the officers wondered to themselves. Jennifer said her parents were divorced and she only saw her father a couple of times a year—usually at Christmas. She had last seen him at her high school graduation. She loved her father and in a few days she would turn eighteen. At that point she could see him anytime she wanted to, Jennifer said. Jennifer did not seem to realize that she was under arrest for capital murder and would not be seeing anyone anytime she wanted. She was still somewhere in her fantasy world. Perhaps a few days in a cell would bring reality up close and personal.

Somewhere along the way the cars stopped at a fast-food

restaurant. The officers went inside, leaving Jennifer and the two boys locked in the cars. Police cars have "cages" in the backseat and no locks or handles inside on the back doors. The teens were secure.

They also were being recorded, but they didn't know. The boys, locked in the backseat of one of the squad cars, chatted about games, smoking and cartoons. David could be heard giggling about Mickey Mouse on the recording. He sounded so young—so childlike. Then David asked Paul about being charged with capital murder as opposed to murder, and Paul explained what he knew about the difference. They chatted a little about Susan.

"I helped her pee," David said, giggling.

He was referring to his mother's release of urine when she died.

There was more talking and giggling. Then: "You dumb Dora," David said, apparently talking about his mother. "You're stupid. We should have stuck her in a big wooden crate and mailed her to a zoo. They'd be like, 'That's an ape?'"

20

Denton County Jail

And so the three teens who had fled Denton County returned in police cars, their dreams of fleeing to Canada dead. It was an eleven-hour trip and the officers took turns driving. Dreaming of who knows what, the prisoners slumped in the backseats as the cars drove steadily south and finally entered Texas. The Roanoke squad car containing the juvenile boys drove to the criminal investigation division building behind the Denton County Jail.

Texas Ranger Tracy Murphree had picked up Justice of the Peace Mike Bateman and he waited in an office there to give Paul Henson Jr. and David Bailey their juvenile rights and to arraign them. Sherrif's Investigator Larry Kish waited with him. Bateman had begun his career as a Denton police officer before running for the lower court office. He and Murphree and Kish all lived in the small Denton County town of Sanger.

Susan played violin in her school orchestra and clarinet in the school band. She was proficient in both instruments, and her mother thought she might become a musician. Instead she graduated from college with a business degree and combined that with her love of pretty clothing to become a clothing-store manager.

Stephen Morten

Susan at a party, around the time she married Richard Bailey in California while he was in the Air Force.

Kate Morten

Kate Morten taught her daughter to sew and quilt as she was growing up, and Susan used the skills to decorate on a budget and also to make some extra money.

Stephen Morten

Officers found Susan's driver's license along with her body and seized it for evidence in her murder.

Jeff Coats

Susan's mother cropped this photo of her daughter from a family picture to use at Susan's memorial service.

Kate Morten

Above: A photo taken of David and Jennifer in happier times.
Kate Morten

Right: David and Jennifer on Jennifer's high school graduation day.
Kate Morten

Susan Bailey took this photo of her children with family members during a visit to Minnesota.
Kate Morten

Right: A crime-scene photo taken in the Bailey house during the initial investigation shows Jennifer Bailey and Paul Henson Jr. at Jennifer's senior prom in 2008.

Jeff Coats

Below: The investigators took this photo of a big hunk of cut hair at the crime scene. They later matched the hair to Paul Henson Jr.

Sharon Baughman

Police found a small baseball bat on Jennifer's bed. They initially suspected it had been used to damage the back of Susan's head, but the autopsy determined that the damage was caused by a knife.

Jeff Coats

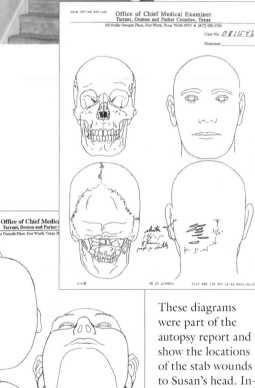

Roanoke police found Susan's body prone just to the left of the staircase on the second floor of her house.

Jeff Coats

These diagrams were part of the autopsy report and show the locations of the stab wounds to Susan's head. Including the wounds to her body, Susan suffered twenty-six stab wounds in all.

Sharon Baughman

After preparing a second search warrant for the house, Larry Kish (left) and Tracy Murphree use a special spray to turn blood smears purple so fingerprints and other evidence will become visible. *Jeff Coats*

Tracy Murphree, Larry Kish and Brian Peterson talked briefly to Jennifer while she was detained in a juvenile facility in Minnesota. *Larry Kish*

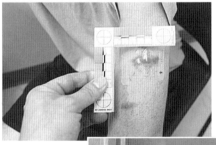

Above: The cut on Paul's arm was evidence that he was a "cutter" and sucked blood from the self-inflicted wound. *Larry Kish*

Right: Paul Henson Jr. in the Stiles Unit near Beaumont, Texas, after his plea bargain and his move to the Texas Department of Criminal Justice. *Donna Fielder*

The Clemens Unit in far South Texas, where David is incarcerated.
Texas Department of Criminal Justice

Left: David Bailey's official mug shot after he became a legal adult and was transferred to the adult prison system.
Texas Department of Criminal Justice

Below: Jennifer in the Mountain View Unit in Gatesville, Texas.
Donna Fielder

Roanoke Detective Brian Peterson, now chief deputy in Somervell County, Texas.
Donna Fielder

Texas Ranger Tracy Murphree, now a candidate for sheriff of Denton County.
Donna Fielder

Denton County Death Investigator Sharon Baughman, now a detective lieutenant with the Cooke County Sheriff's Office.
Donna Fielder

Bateman was surprised when he saw a small boy with a sweet face walk in the back door of the building accompanied by an older teen and the two Roanoke officers. He looked at Kish and Murphree. *That was David Bailey*, the officers confirmed. The elfin boy looked no more than ten years old, but they knew he was thirteen.

"Son, do you know why you are being held by the police?" Bateman asked the boy.

David smiled brightly.

"For the capital murder of my mother," he said.

The men looked at one another. They were almost speechless at the answer. Finally, Bateman gave both the boys the legal notifications for juveniles, and the Roanoke officers led them out the door and back into the car.

Bateman looked at Kish and Murphree.

"That ain't right," he said sardonically.

It was like a scene out of a horror movie, Murphree thought. The small stature of the boy, the childish smile and the total evil of the words he'd spoken. Just scary.

The officers processed both boys into their cells in the juvenile section of the jail. South Dakota jailers had turned over their property, the clothing and other things they were carrying with them, in a plastic bag. The Denton County officers prepared the bags for safekeeping in the juvenile area. Among the things in Paul's bag was a necklace with a vial containing what appeared to be blood.

MAGISTRATE'S WARNING
TO CHILD OFFENDER

This is to certify that before me, the undersigned magistrate of the State of Texas, County of Denton, personally appeared David Bailey who states that he is 13 years of age, and in the custody of Brian Peterson, a law enforcement officer with the Roanoke Police Department. Acting in my official capacity as a magistrate for the State of Texas, I hereby give the following warnings:

(1) You are in custody because it is alleged that you have committed the offense of CAPITAL MURDER;

A. You may remain silent and not make any statement at all and that any statement you make may be used in evidence against you;

B. You have the right to have an attorney present to advise you either prior to any questioning or during the questioning;

C. If you are unable to employ an attorney, you have the right to have an attorney appointed to counsel with you prior to or during any interviews with peace officers or attorneys representing the state; and

D. You have the right to terminate the interview at any time.

IN WITNESS THEREOF I have officially subscribed
my hand this 1st day of October 2008, at 10:19 P.M.

Mike Bateman
Justice of the Peace Pct. #5

(David Bailey) Child's Signature

The two boys were driven to the Denton County Juvenile Detention Center, which lies just behind the main jail,
and they were booked in. They refused to talk to investigators. Obviously, they had all sworn to keep silent.

Jennifer, riding in the second Roanoke squad car, was
taken to the female section of the main jail. At seventeen,
she was an adult and would be treated as one. A jailer began
asking questions for the book-in documentation. He asked
for her cellular telephone number.

"I don't have my cell anymore," she said.

The jailer asked her where it was, although he had been
told by other officers that the kids had thrown their phones
in the bathtub. He wanted to see what she would say. She
had thrown it in a bathtub full of water, she answered. She
didn't tell him that they'd all thrown their phones in the
water in hopes of erasing anything incriminating in e-mails
or text messages, and that they hadn't taken them along
because they believed they could be traced by the cellular
signals.

"We were in a hurry and we didn't take anything
with us."

The jailer asked for her home telephone number.

Jennifer shrugged. "There's pretty much no one there lately," she said.

Her casual attitude was chilling. But it was bravado.

Jennifer was booked and led to a protective custody cell block containing eight cells. Catwalks ran around the block and through it, allowing jailers to watch over the inmates. One female jailer found Jennifer alone in a cell. She was sobbing.

"What's the matter?" the jailer asked the teen.

"I want my mom," Jennifer sobbed.

"Well, we have visitation, and she can come and see you soon," said the jailer, pretending not to know what crime Jennifer was accused of.

Jennifer just turned over and sobbed louder. All through the night, the jailer checked on the girl, who never stopped crying.

Kate's Journal

Sunday, September 29, 2008

Numb. Not much sleep. Sad sad sad—[son-in-law] very upset with kids. Will have nothing to do with them. They are murderers.

21

More Search Warrants

The officers conferred often. There was much to be done. Texas is a death penalty state, but it takes a lot of evidence to convince a jury to find that a defendant should be executed. As Ranger Tracy Murphree had said, it may have been Jennifer's first murder, but it wasn't the first for most of the officers. It may have been Roanoke's first homicide, but it wasn't the first in Denton County by any means.

The county has a rich history of famous lawbreakers, going back to the wild days when the land first was settled. In the mid-1880s, Denton County's best-known criminal was Sam Bass, subject of legend and even a song. Bass worked for a while as a stable hand for Denton County Sheriff William Egan but he loved horse racing, which was illegal. Sheriff Egan couldn't take the heat of having one of his employees winning money on illegal bets. So he let him go. Soon Bass was rustling cattle, holding up stagecoaches and robbing trains. The Texas Rangers killed Sam Bass on his twenty-seventh birthday in Round Rock, Texas, in 1878. A monument marks the place where they shot him.

Bass wasn't the only Texas outlaw to become famous in popular lore. Bonnie Parker and Clyde Barrow were Depression-era robbers from Dallas who had sometimes hidden out in areas of Denton County and had knocked over a few nearby banks. They killed a number of law enforcement officers, but the Rangers put a sudden, violent end to them in Louisiana in 1934. They lived again on the big screen, and the movie *Bonnie and Clyde*, starring Warren Beatty and Faye Dunaway, was filmed largely in Denton County, and had its world premiere at the Campus Theatre in Denton in 1967.

Cattle baron Rex Cauble went to federal prison in 1982 on federal racketeering charges in connection with the discovery of an entire shrimp boat full of marijuana on a boat he owned. Cauble swore his innocence until the day he died in 2003. His famous show barn, where his party guests had included Clark Gable, still is visible, slowly rusting into ruin, from Interstate 35 in northern Denton County.

Serial killer Henry Lee Lucas killed his teenage common-law wife, Becky, in Denton in 1982. He later confessed to more than three hundred murders but later recanted and said he'd only killed his mother.

More recently, two punks just paroled from prison found two teenagers looking for a place to be alone north of Denton. In 1993, Cari Crews and Jesus Garza were murdered at Clear Creek with a sawed-off shotgun the men had stolen from a pickup truck. Cari had been raped. James Lee Clark and James Richard Brown were charged with capital murder.

Clark was convicted and executed, and Brown served twenty years in prison for aggravated robbery.

The county made national news again in 2002, when Denton police detective Bobby Lozano shot and killed his wife in Denton. Because the first indictment against him was dropped, Lozano walked free until seven years later, when he was found guilty on a subsequent indictment and sentenced to forty-five years in prison.

But no criminals had been as young as Jennifer, Paul and David. No crime had been so personal, so planned, so ugly. On Friday, October 3, 2008, Murphree prepared affidavits for search warrants to take samples of blood, hair and buccal swabs (swabbing the mouth with cotton to collect DNA from cheek cells) for each of the three teens. Medical personnel from the Denton County Jail took the samples from Jennifer. Medical personnel from the juvenile detention center took samples from Paul and David. All the samples were turned over to Kish, who took them to the Texas Department of Public Safety lab to be tested.

Roanoke police received a call from a neighbor of the Baileys on Oxford Drive on October 4. He had been concerned because the grass in the yard was getting high, he said, so he had sought and received permission to mow the grass. In the backyard, he had discovered two knives lying about five feet apart in the tall grass. An officer responded and took possession of the knives and placed them into evidence. Murphree didn't believe they had been used in the actual crime. They looked as though they had been used in practice throwing, he thought. He envisioned the kids out in the backyard with the knives, sharpening up their knife techniques.

On Monday, October 6, Murphree prepared search warrant affidavits for the homes of Paul Henson and Merrilee White. That day, after the warrants were signed by Judge Bruce McFarling, Murphree, Kish, Coats and Peterson drove to unincorporated Denton County, just outside the Haslet city limits, to search Paul Henson Sr.'s house.

Up a long driveway they found a single-wide mobile home. On one side lay a flat-bottomed boat, and two pickup trucks were parked on the other side. They noticed an old-fashioned television antenna and a window air conditioner. They served the warrant and began their search. The mobile home was clean and furnished with moderately nice furniture, but it was cluttered with more property than there was room to put away neatly. All over the long, narrow building the walls were lined with family photographs. In Paul's bedroom the bed was made. The windows were darkened with black curtains and the spread was gray. He had a small television set and stereo speakers. On the wall over the bed hung a handmade poster with the letters "P" and "J" surrounded by hearts. His shelves were very neat. On them the officers saw a big book titled *Fragon*. It apparently was about a fantasy character that was half frog and half dragon. A quote associated with the book reads, "Thou shalt not taunt thy fragon, for thou shalt become homosexual or dead or both."

The items on the bookshelf were interesting. There were "cards of destiny" and tarot cards. On the stack of tarot cards, the card depicting the devil lay on top. The prom photo the officers had seen in the Bailey house also hung on Paul's bedroom wall and a second copy was taped to a computer monitor. They seized two computers from the house. They took several handwritten notes written to and from Paul discussing a "plan" and "going to Canada." In his closet they found big boxes advertising that they contained musical and illuminated wizards and dragons.

In Paul's room they found but did not seize a strange-looking device that turned out to be a "Fleshlight." On the outside, it looked a bit like a flashlight, and Paul Sr. had no idea what it really was—which was an "artificial vagina," made as a masturbatory aid. (Later, when the officers asked Paul Jr. about it, he told them that Merrilee had purchased it for him using her mother's credit card. The officers were bemused. Here was a sixteen-year-old boy who was having sex with two pretty young women and he still needed an artificial vagina?)

In a three-ring notebook binder the officers found a number of photocopied pages titled *The Demonic Bible*. The author was listed as "Magus Tsirk Susez, Antichrist, servant and disciple of the dark lord as revealed to him by his unholy demon the spirit Azael."

"If power corrupts and absolute power corrupts absolutely, then the omnipotent creator of Heaven and earth must be the most evil son-of-a-bitch who ever lived," it began.

The book was self-important in tone and written in such dense language that it would be difficult for any sixteen-year-old boy to understand much of it. It discussed magic and mysticism, demons and devils. It was not the entire *Demonic Bible*, which is thousands of pages long, claimed the book.

The author claimed the original was "written upon parchment made from human flesh, in ink made from human blood in a strange, alien script." It gave instructions for a purification ceremony that involved dressing in black, bathing in salt water and reciting the Lord's Prayer backward three times. It offered the keys to "crossing the gates of Hell and becoming one with the forces of darkness."

The one who would be purified had to announce, "I renounce all that is holy and all that is good and I proclaim that Satan Lucifer is god of the earth."

It offered chants for invoking Beelzebub, demons and other evil things. It contained a ritual to become the devil incarnate. There also was a ritual to become a vampire. And a general invocation for calling spirits: "I call all the forces of darkness into myself," would invoke evil spirits, the book claimed.

Well, the officers thought, *that part seemed to have worked for Paul*. The officers took it with them.

Peterson took the binder to his office and read through it. It was alternately chilling and just plain silly. Another Roanoke officer walked up to Peterson's desk and asked what he was reading. It was Paul's demonic bible, Peterson told him.

"Petey, I wouldn't read that," the officer said with concern.

"It's part of the investigation," Peterson said.

"Still, I'd just leave it alone."

"I'm not worried about a bogyman," Peterson said. "I've read the Bible all the way through, and we win."

When dealing with such tragedy and such evil, it was necessary to develop a wicked sense of humor.

Evidence continued to come in from several places. Fort Worth police turned over to Peterson a letter intercepted from Merrilee addressed to Paul that she'd written while in the juvenile center there. She wrote that she'd heard what happened and was sorry. She hadn't been able to meet them on Tuesday as they'd planned, she said, because she'd gotten arrested and taken to the Tarrant County Juvenile Detention Center. She was still there, she wrote.

She didn't care which one of them killed Susan Bailey, she wrote. What she couldn't figure out was why they didn't leave on Tuesday as they'd planned. She thought she had missed their departure when she was arrested, and then she learned they had not left until Thursday night. Why had they waited? Had they never planned to take her along as they promised?

"Everything you told me. Everything I saw. Was it all a lie?"

Merrilee was confused because she thought they were all going to leave on the day she was arrested, but she heard that Susan was found dead the following Sunday.

"Ya'all didn't stick to the plan and now ya'all are in big trouble. I wish you luck."

She signed the letter "Doom Kitten."

The officers were convinced that there had been a conspiracy to kill all their parents and it was all supposed to happen at once on Tuesday. But Merrilee had been caught, and that threw their plans into chaos. It wasn't like they had been well-formed plans to begin with. The plan was sort of like, *Okay, let's kill our parents, drive to Canada and live happily ever after.* These were criminal minds at work, clearly, but they were also really young minds.

"They planned, but they were still kids. They left all the evidence there. If they had hidden the evidence or had taken it away, it would have been much harder for us to figure out what happened. The whole case still bothers me," Kish said years later. "You try not to personalize it, but it's hard. I have three children, and I can't imagine them even thinking about doing such a thing."

"They may have thought they had the whole deal ready," Coats added. "But this was not the perfect crime."

On October 2, 2008, a Fort Worth detective had called Merrilee's mother, Amy White. He told her he wanted to talk about the situation that had occurred at her house on September 23. Amy told him that she didn't think she should talk to him without her lawyer.

"You're not a suspect, ma'am," he replied.

Well, she had hired a lawyer for her daughter, Merrilee, and she would feel better if he were present, she said. The detective again explained that suspects had the right to an attorney. But Amy was a victim. She had called 911 for help.

"You can hang up, but there is no reason for an attorney," he said.

Finally, reluctantly, Amy agreed to talk to him. Merrilee had run away on September 19, 2008. Amy had checked at Jennifer Bailey's house but was told that her daughter was not there. She later learned that Merrilee had been hiding upstairs. On September 22, she found her daughter walking down a street in Roanoke and took her home. Merrilee was defiant and upset and Amy had called police to get her under control.

Then, the next morning, she awoke to find her daughter hovering over her with a butcher knife drawn back as if she were going to stab her. She crawled to the other side of the bed to get away and then called 911. By the time officers arrived she had the knife, Amy said.

"She told me she wasn't going to hurt me," Amy said. "She threw the knife down."

"Do you think her intent was to kill you?"

"No, I don't. I think she was not in her right mind. She was saying that Paul was her scarecrow god. She was not normal. I seriously believe they brainwashed her."

It became clear to the detective that Amy had lapsed into protective-mother mode. She downplayed the incident with the knife. Since the time of that incident, the tragic events of September 25, 2008, had taken place. There had been a plan to kill parents, and one of them was dead. What did she know about that? the officer asked the mom.

Merrilee was not aware of any plot to kill Susan Bailey, Amy was adamant.

Later that day, the detective received a telephone call from Shane White*, Merrilee's stepfather. He said he had come over the night Merrilee was found after running away and that she'd been very upset. He'd called the next morning to talk about Merrilee's homework, and Amy said that she was fending off Merrilee, who had a knife. He'd been the one to tell Amy to hang up and call the police, he said, though Amy had not mentioned talking to him during the attack. Later, he learned that Merrilee had been detained and was in juvenile hall.

But Shane's main objective for calling the detective now seemed to be to learn the depth of the trouble that Merrilee was in. He had learned the charge was aggravated assault, family violence. But then he heard that it had been aggravated

* Denotes pseudonym

robbery because she was trying to get the car. He was confused, he said. How many charges was she actually facing?

The detective explained that the robbery charge had been applied by the original officers and then withdrawn.

"It's hard to rob someone you live with," he said.

So was there anything in the charge against her about taking the car?

The detective said no. Shane White told him that he had learned that Merrilee had planned to go with Jennifer and Paul when they drove to Canada. That's why she attacked her mother. She wasn't trying to hurt her; she just wanted the car so she could go with her friends, he explained.

"Is she going to be linked to that other situation?"

The "other situation" he was talking about was the murder of Susan Bailey. That was not in the detective's jurisdiction. Any information he had about that was not going to be passed on to the parent of one of the teens involved.

"I don't know. Do you think she had the intent to kill Amy?"

There was a pause.

"I honestly don't know," the stepfather said.

Later, on October 6, the officers served a search warrant at the White home in Fort Worth. The two-story home lay in an affluent neighborhood and was a far cry from the simple trailer where Paul lived. The house was pristine, furnished elegantly. The walls were a fashionable creamy color with a lighter cream on the woodwork. The kitchen was done in dark wood and granite with black appliances. Real plants softened the rooms, which were decorated with art.

In one bedroom a stack of board games like Scrabble

and Bunco lay on the bed. Nowhere was there a hint that in this house a fourteen-year-old girl had tried to stab her mother. Except, maybe, in a drawer in Merrilee's room. The officers found a big spiral notebook with the word "vampire" colored in letters that covered a page. Also in that drawer was the Northwest Independent School District ID tag of another girl. There was a mystery about those student identification cards. The officers had found Merrilee's and Paul's ID cards at Jennifer's house. Now another girl's card lay in Merrilee's bedside table drawer. Was it fashionable to trade ID cards? They never found out.

Merrilee's room featured a black four-poster bed with a black spread covered with big hot pink flowers. A few stuffed toys showed that in some ways Merrilee was still a child. On her wall was a tasteful plaque. It read: "My daughter, you've blessed my life greatly. I'm so glad we are friends . . . The time we have together is the best that I spend."

Merrilee's mother, Amy White, was a beautiful dark-haired woman who seemed to just want the trouble that had entered her life to go away. She'd heartily disapproved of her daughter having anything to do with Paul. She'd sensed that he was a bad influence on the younger teen, and she really didn't know much about Jennifer either. Merrilee and Jennifer appeared to be close friends, despite the difference in their ages. But when Merrilee went missing, both Jennifer and Paul had claimed to have no idea where her daughter might be. Were they lying? Amy thought so, but she hadn't known how to overcome the lies to find her daughter. She'd driven around Roanoke looking for Merrilee and placing signs in public places asking people to call if they saw her.

She then spotted her daughter walking down the street. She stopped and ordered her into the car. The girl got in, but all the while cried and talked about sharing past lives with Jennifer and Paul. That really scared her, Amy said.

Merrilee wasn't making sense and she was overwrought. Amy said she tried to calm her but finally had to call the police to get the situation under control. She had thought things were all right when she went to bed with Merrilee crying in the next room. But the next morning she awoke to find Merrilee standing over her with a knife held above her head as though she were going to stab her, Amy said. Merrilee demanded the car keys and money. She had to go with Paul and Jennifer, she said. The mother was able to get the knife away from Merrilee and call police. The officers took her daughter away, but Merrilee would not have harmed her, she was sure of that, Amy White claimed. Amy loved her daughter and attributed her strange behavior to the company she had been keeping. Her daughter was not a killer, she insisted. She would never have hurt her mother.

The officers were not so sure of that, given the butcher knife that Merrilee had been wielding and the role butcher knives had played in the death of Susan Bailey—another mother who never dreamed her daughter would harm her.

Later, Murphree reviewed the Fort Worth police report on the incident at the White house. It contained sparse information and little that he didn't already know. The only thing Merrilee had told the officers at the time, according to the report, was that she was going to take the car and a couple of friends to Canada. And she had told them that if Paul had a gun, then "the plan" was going down.

Kate's Journal

Tuesday, October 7, 2008

Police said before Susan figured out what was happening to her she was dead—happened fast—thank God!

22

What to Do?

Everything was confusion at the Morten house. Kate and Stephen were in shock. Their daughter was dead. Their grandchildren were in custody, charged with the capital crime of killing her. They really didn't want their neighbors to know what their grandkids had done. But they would have to explain the death of their daughter some way. They talked about it but could come up with no good answer. Would there be a service in Minnesota or should they plan the service for Texas? Kate discussed the issues with her other daughter and her two sons. The medical examiner had asked for the name of a funeral home near Roanoke where the body could be taken once the autopsy was finished. Kate had no idea what to tell them. She didn't know the names of any funeral homes in Texas.

Her children began to help. They called a local funeral home for advice and learned the name of a Denton, Texas, mortuary they could use. They began calling relatives to let them know what had happened. They rehashed what they knew over and over until Kate could hardly bear listening. But it became clear to her that a memorial service in their hometown was needed.

The children said it was unreasonable to pay the high price of flying Susan's body up to Minnesota and buying a cemetery plot. As a family, they decided cremation was the best option. They would have it done in Texas. But they would have a memorial service before leaving for their daughter's home. They wanted that done with.

Meanwhile, calls began coming in. Susan's supervisor at the dress store in Texas was brokenhearted, she said. It was all over the news in Dallas. So much for keeping the kids' role a secret. Some of the media already had obtained results of the search warrant on the Bailey house and listed the items taken. Why would they do that? It seemed such an invasion of Susan's privacy to put a list of her seized belongings on the news.

And Kate couldn't help herself. She continued to call Roanoke police to check on her grandchildren. One part of her brain accepted the fact that they had murdered her daughter. But another part of her mind still loved Jennifer and David and could not accept the fact that they had stabbed their mother. It was all so overwhelming. How could her grandchildren have done such a thing to her daughter? It was beyond her understanding. Kate couldn't stop crying, and she wasn't sure whom she was crying for the most.

A daughter-in-law agreed to make a picture board for

the local memorial service. Kate went through all her photos and found the ones she wanted to use. It made her feel close to Susan to go through the boxes of pictures showing her childhood, her young womanhood and her later life. She wanted to put Susan's wedding picture on a board, she said. But cut off the half with Richard on it, she directed.

In the midst of all the planning, Kate stopped to realize that that day was supposed to have been Jennifer's first at college.

On Thursday, October 2, 2008, the Mortens met with friends at the church for the service. It was filled with the sweet scent of flowers. Bouquets surrounded the three photo boards filled with family pictures displaying Susan's activities. They arrived at two P.M. though the service was not supposed to start until three P.M. Already, people were arriving and Kate began to greet them. Time passed and people became a bit restless. The pastor was late and the funeral director was unhappy. Finally, the service began and the pastor's wife played songs that Kate loved. The pastor's wife tried to sing but broke down and Kate rose and hugged her. The service was emotional. Friends came from everywhere, even the Arizona town where she and Stephen spent their winters. One neighbor came who had undergone triple bypass surgery a day earlier.

"I am overwhelmed by the support," Kate wrote in her journal.

She listed pages of names of the people who came to share the memory of her daughter. It was a day of remembering, she wrote.

The next day Kate began making plans to drive to Texas.

Already exhausted, she dreaded going. But one of her sons learned the house had been released to the family after a forensic cleaning. He made a call and had the locks changed. They would first go to the Roanoke Police Department, and officers would accompany them to the house when they saw it for the first time. They would go through the house to determine what they would bring back to Minnesota and what they would do with the rest. It was a large house with a lot of furniture and decorations. It would be a big job. They briefly talked about staying in the house but didn't think that they could do it, so they made reservations in a hotel near Roanoke. Between paying for the cremation, for several days in hotels on the way down and then in Roanoke—as well as on the trip back—and with gasoline prices so high, Kate worried about all the expense.

Susan's ex, Richard Bailey, already had gone to Yankton to pick up her car, Kate learned. The dog had been impounded and she never learned what happened to it after that. She could not find anyone who knew what happened to the cat. Richard had planned to attend his children's arraignment, but the police up there told him to stay away.

Sunday, October 5, 2008, was Jennifer's eighteenth birthday. Kate and Stephen in their van and their daughter and son-in-law in a Suburban were on the road to Roanoke. By the time they checked into their first motel on the road, Kate was exhausted.

The next day was David's fourteenth birthday. Kate remembered the boy who spent the summer with her and grieved for that boy, who was now charged with capital murder. That was not the child she knew. But in the back of her mind lingered the memory of the boy who had neared violence when he didn't get the snorkel he wanted.

They arrived at the funeral home in Denton at eleven A.M. Susan's ashes were ready. It was a small box that held her daughter, who had been large, Kate thought.

Then the four drove to the Roanoke Police Department to meet Detective Brian Peterson and Sergeant Chris Almonrode. Peterson embraced Kate and told her that he had the upmost respect for Susan. He told them about the officers' search for Paul several days earlier and finding the butcher knife under the couch cushion. He said that Susan and Jennifer had argued over Paul that day.

The detectives told the family about Jennifer's friend Merrilee White. They had found her prescription medication and her school identification card in Susan's house. That same Tuesday that Roanoke police were looking for Paul, Merrilee's mother had called Fort Worth police because her daughter was threatening her with a knife. The girl was being held in juvenile detention in Tarrant County, they said. They believed Merrilee was involved in the plot, the detectives said. They were not sure just how far her involvement went, but they intended to find out. Merrilee was only fourteen. These kids were all so young!

Almonrode told the family that he had taught David in an after-school class. David was a great kid, the sergeant said. He could tell that he came from a good, hardworking home. He didn't understand what had happened.

Neither did Kate.

Then the Roanoke officers escorted the family to the house at The Parks of Roanoke. There were vases of flowers in the driveway from neighbors. No reporters lurked around the house, but the Mortens quickly went inside. Reporters had been a problem for the neighbors, and the officers suspected they would come again when they learned that family was in the house. Kate decided that it felt okay in her daughter's home—not eerie—but she was not ready to go upstairs.

Kate could see that the first order of business would be to clean. Some of the surfaces were covered in something purple. Almonrode explained that came from the investigation. Blood turned that purple color when sprayed with a special substance, and the detectives had sprayed it all over the house, especially upstairs. Kate's daughter and son-in-law wanted proof of everything that happened. They took pictures of everything. They would take more pictures when the house was empty, they said.

The four went to work. They threw out bowls of moldy food and cartons of soured milk. They threw out the watermelon rind. They rewashed clothing that had been in the washing machine and had dried. They used a bleach solution to clean off the purple dye. That was hard work.

Vacuuming was slow going. The bag filled so fast with dirt and cat hair. Kate remembered vacuuming the house herself when she was there for Jennifer's graduation. Jennifer had been told to do the chore and swore she did. But the rugs were dirty, and Kate had known she was lying.

"Shame on those kids," she wrote in her journal. "They never lifted a finger to help at home."

She and Stephen were back at the house early the next day. Alone for a few minutes, they both sat down and cried.

Then they returned to the task of washing things and bagging and boxing them. Some they would take home. Others would be given to charity. They knew they could not just leave the house in this condition.

At two P.M. that day they met with a probate lawyer. He told them to use any of Susan's assets to pay her debts. As for the house and any debt that could not be covered, let it slide, he told them.

"Susan would end up with bad credit," Kate wrote in her journal. "Do we care? No."

After they returned to the house, Sheryl Barnes, Susan's friend and neighbor from around the corner, came to the door. She told them that she and Susan had moved to the neighborhood at about the same time. Their children had been about the same ages, and they had grown close.

Sheryl wanted to plan a memorial service for Susan in Roanoke, and told them that she would take care of the details. She knew a pastor in the neighborhood who would perform the service. Sheryl also told them about a Christian donation site nearby, and they loaded up the Suburban with a pile of newly washed clothing and dropped it off.

Kate noted her son-in-law, her older daughter's husband, was throwing anything that belonged to Jennifer or David out on the curb. Bed headboards, dressers, their clothing. They could hardly stand to touch anything that belonged to the kids. Her son-in-law assumed the city would pick it up there on trash day but some police officers came by to tell them that they could not leave anything on the curb. The officers showed them a Dumpster where they could put the things they didn't want to keep. They made several trips.

Finally, Kate gathered her courage and walked up the stairs. The hallway in front of Jennifer's door had been stripped of carpet, and Kilz paint sealer covered the sub-flooring there. She knew it was there to seal off her daughter's blood. The door to Jennifer's room had been removed. This was the place where her daughter had died. She felt a chill.

She stepped carefully past the stripped spot and looked into the other rooms. Here was more, much more, work to do. The purple substance was everywhere. The tub in Susan's bath was dark, dark purple and there were tiles cut out of the splashboard and Sheetrock cut out of the walls. Kate felt eerie in that bathroom. She could not bring herself to go near the tub.

23

Peterson's Investigation

Detective Brian Peterson interviewed the Mortens at the police department. Kate did much of the talking. Stephen sat quietly and interjected occasionally. They were neatly dressed and calm. They talked about their former son-in-law first. They didn't like him. He was self-centered and had been verbally abusive to Susan and both kids, they said. He didn't work much. When Susan had told her mother a year before the split-up that she was planning to divorce him, Kate had been glad. And she had been even happier when the divorce was final around Christmas two years earlier. The grandkids had flown to Arizona to spend the holiday with them, she recalled.

Jennifer and her mother had had a good relationship until she started dating Paul, her grandmother said. They went shopping together and Susan took her kids to the movies. Kate said that once her granddaughter started dating Paul,

Jennifer seemed to live in a fantasy world that was part the books she read and part the games she was playing. She'd also lied to her mother about her job at a fast-food place. She hadn't been working there any longer but claimed she was.

Kate said she'd spoken by telephone to Jennifer on the Tuesday before the murder. Jennifer claimed that she had a job doing online surveys for some kind of teddy bear website. It paid a hundred dollars a day, she'd claimed. Her grandmother hadn't believed her.

Peterson told the Mortens that there were things he needed to tell them that they would not enjoy hearing. But those things would come out in court at the children's trials and he didn't want them to find out that way. He needed to tell them how Susan had died and why he believed their grandchildren did it.

"They are ugly and they will hurt," he warned them of these details. "But I want justice for Susan."

He told them the investigation so far showed that all three teens were involved in stabbing Susan.

"We were hoping David was not involved," Kate said.

"When I first walked in that house, I thought, 'Dear God, surely not David.' But I believe he was involved," Peterson told them. "I believe the kids did it."

"She loved those kids. She protected them. She worked hard for them," Kate protested.

Peterson said he believed Susan's death was very quick and that she didn't suffer.

He told the Mortens of the evidence he had found that tied Susan's children to her death. He was gentle about describing the murder itself and the condition he'd found their daughter in. Brian Peterson was a compassionate man, and he had personally known Susan.

Kate passed on the story of finding Jennifer and Paul nearly naked in the girl's locked bedroom when she came for her granddaughter's graduation. She was so angry that Jennifer would dishonor her like that. But that was nothing compared to what Jennifer had done to her own mother.

Peterson told them about the girl in Fort Worth who'd also tried to stab her mother. They were investigating the depth of her involvement with the plot to kill Susan. She apparently was part of the conspiracy and might be tried as a coconspirator.

He tried to comfort Susan's parents. They were quiet and restrained. But they were hurting badly, he surmised. He handed them a card with all his telephone numbers on it.

"I don't care when or where you call me," he told them in a kindly voice. "I will tell you anything I know. Call me anytime you need me. It won't bother me at all."

Peterson also asked Paul Henson Sr., Paul's father, to come in for an interview.

Paul Sr. was a burly guy, and he showed up in work boots, faded jeans and a plaid shirt with the sleeves cut off at the shoulders. His hair was longish and slicked back under a "gimme cap." Paul Sr. asked if it was OK if he recorded the interview, and Peterson assented. Peterson even told him that he had a nice voice recorder. And then ensued a long, detailed discussion about John Wayne movies.

Peterson knew he needed to build rapport with this man, and he was willing to talk about the Duke, Ringo Kid and Rooster Cogburn for as long as Paul Sr. wanted.

They finally got around to talking about Paul Jr., whom the father called JR.

JR was a quiet kid who was good with computers, Paul Sr. said. He played video games and watched a lot of TV. Read? Just computer code books. JR didn't have a car but his dad was looking to buy him a '77 Chevy Nova. They'd do the work themselves to get it running, he said. He was basically a good kid who sometimes skipped class "like all kids do," he said. Once he ran away with a friend to Burleson but the police brought him home.

JR had been dating Jennifer about a year, Paul Sr. said. He met Jennifer's mom, Susan, once, and she was weird about the two dating each other.

"She had wishy-washy feelings on that. One time she's okay and the next not."

Jennifer had run away eight or nine times, Paul Sr. said. More than once he had walked into JR's bedroom and found her there. He would take her home the next morning. She didn't like to babysit her brother and didn't think she should have to watch him while her mother was at work. She and JR had talked about getting married and moving into the trailer with him and his wife, Paul Sr. said.

"But I think JR was kind of a Romeo. I found several notes from different girls. Just kid notes, you know."

Peterson asked him if he knew about the *Demonic Bible* in his son's room. No, and he didn't believe that JR was into anything like that. Oh, once he did find a deck of tarot cards, but those had belonged to Jennifer, Paul Sr. said.

He was shocked that Paul Jr. had cut off his long hair. It had been a source of pride to his son. It had not been cut in a long time and JR wouldn't let anybody near it with a pair of scissors. He said he'd talked to his son while he was in South Dakota, and JR had denied having anything to do with the murder.

"I asked him if he knew about Jennifer's mother. He said 'what?' and he got deathly quiet. I told him flat-out you don't talk to nobody till you get back here and get an attorney."

Paul Sr. said he thought that Jennifer "lured" Paul to her house and cut his hair for some reason. Maybe Susan came home and saw that and became angry, he said. Maybe Susan ran him out of the house. Maybe Jennifer stabbed her mother after Paul was out of the house.

"He gave the position he was not involved. That he was out of that house and she came out—'Let's go, let's go!' I think (Susan) ran him out of the house and then things exploded. I think he tried to be her protector—trying to help her out."

"He needs to try to help himself out," Peterson said. "You ever heard of him drinking blood?"

"Huh. He don't."

Was his father sure about that?

"Well, a long time ago he used to make cuts on his arms and suck on it. I think he did it to scare people and it was actually catsup."

Peterson asked about the pistol. Paul Sr. thought his son took it to sell it since he didn't have any money.

"I used it to kill snakes—cottonmouths," he said.

The two men talked about snakes for a while.

Paul Sr. wanted to know about his son's charges. There seemed to be a lot of them, and he didn't understand. All those charges—they worried him. Peterson explained that

Paul Jr., at sixteen, was still legally a juvenile. Peterson was required to list anything that would qualify as delinquent behavior, like running away and stealing Susan's car. There was a lot of that, but the other things were small stuff.

"He is only charged with capital murder," Peterson said with a straight face. "You have my word."

He was hoping to have his son home soon, Paul Sr. said. He was very concerned about this whole thing. He was worried about JR.

"The person I'm working for right now is a woman who died a horrible death," Peterson said. "If he didn't do it, I want to clear him. But if he did do it, I want him to be a man so we can take care of this thing."

Peterson left that interview shaking his head. Good police interviewers know they need to build rapport with interviewees before they get down to business. They need to get them to relax, to loosen up, so they will talk more freely. The detective chuckled as he talked to officers who had been listening to the interview on a recorder.

"That's the first time I ever used John Wayne to build rapport," he told them. "But that was the only thing I came upon that we had in common."

Richard Bailey came into the Roanoke police department for an interview dressed in shorts and a sleeveless "muscle" shirt. He was anxious to get some of his property out of the house and had not been allowed to do that, he began. He asked the detective to help him. Peterson explained that property ownership was a civil matter, and he could not help with that. He was working on a murder.

In answer to the officer's questions, Richard said that

he and Susan had been married for eighteen years and divorced for two. Susan yelled a lot, he said. If the kids didn't do exactly what she asked them to do, she yelled. She yelled at him when he wasn't working. The first year they were in Texas he had a job, he said. He'd also been attending a technical school. But he lost the job and he had just come into an inheritance, so he didn't get another job. His father gave him money to help out.

When they were in California, his father had kept the kids for them, Richard said. The elder Bailey had recently died, and Richard cried when he spoke of him. He shed no tears for Susan, however.

Jennifer was a "good kid" until she started dating Paul, her father said. She loved to read and draw, and so did David. Richard said he never met Paul, but he knew there was a lot of fighting in the house because of him. Susan didn't want her daughter to date Paul but Jennifer would not listen to her.

"She told me she was in love with him."

Peterson thought about the interviews that night. Both men were in denial. Each father blamed the murder on the other father's child. Peterson believed that all three teens had been involved in Susan's death. These men were going to have to get a grip, he thought. They were going to have to face the fact that their flesh and blood had committed murder.

Peterson continued to research tidbits of information that various friends had given about the four teens and their plans. He could not determine exactly when David had become part of the conspiracy. Had he known all along what was planned for his mother? Or had he been at home at the wrong time and just fallen in with the plot? Had he really wanted to see his mother dead? Peterson suspected that Jennifer was the instigator. She was the planner. She was the one who'd wanted her mother out of the way. The investigator thought that Paul had probably been the one responsible for most of the major stab wounds, but he believed that the other two stabbed Susan as well. Those five superficial wounds on Susan's chest, for example. David wanted to fit in. He wanted to be part of the plan. But he was hesitant and fearful. So it would make sense that he made a show of cutting his mother with very little actual damage. It did appear that David had been part of the conspiracy. Peterson believed that the boy had known about the plan to stab his mother for quite a while. He had been the one to bicycle to the store for the cleaning product. David was young, but he was not innocent.

He could imagine Paul pulling the knife across Susan's throat. Very little held her head on after those two savage cuts. And the wounds to her back had severed the spinal cord, rendering her helpless. If those had been the first thrusts, they could have done the rest at their leisure. He didn't like to think of that. This homicide had been up close and very personal. It showed a lot of rage. Peterson remembered sitting across from Susan at her kitchen table and the straightforward way she had handled the investigation into some possible sexual abuse of David. He respected that woman. He respected the way she handled her tough life and her financial problems. He hated the memory of her lying in her hallway in her socks and jeans with her bloody Bed Bath & Beyond pin hanging on her blouse.

The lab report on the chocolate pudding came in. It showed that the pudding was laced with an over-the-counter painkiller—a lot of it. So the kids had first tried to poison Susan with a load of crushed medications. She had suspected that after she tasted it, had mentioned it when the officers were there looking for Paul. But she hadn't realized the real danger she was in. She didn't realize that it didn't stop there. All over the house, they had been prepared to kill her.

He thought about the butcher knife hidden under the couch cushion and a second big knife under Jennifer's bed. He thought about the two knives found in the grass toward the back of the lot, and the four knives in Paul's suitcase. Paul had been carrying another pocketknife when he was detained in South Dakota. The boy seemed to have a thing for knives. Then there was the baseball bat, handy on Jennifer's bed. And the frayed electrical cord draped over the shower curtain rod. Too bad they had not tried that first, he thought. The shock would not have been strong enough to harm her, but she might've been alerted to their homicidal intent.

There were clues to what the kids planned. But what mother would truly imagine that her own children were seriously plotting her death?

Susan had not paid attention. She had not given close supervision to her children. Kids need supervision, and this was a horrible example of what could happen when they weren't watched closely enough. But was that really Susan's fault? She was working two jobs and taking in sewing to try to support her family. She obviously never had much financial support from Richard. Was Susan to blame for the time she spent away from home earning money to support her family? Peterson didn't think so. She was doing what she had to do.

He learned the teens favored a style of music called emo, which was a style of rock music that often featured emotional, even confessional lyrics that were sometimes about sadness, pain and suicide. One of their favorite groups was Insane Clown Posse, a duo from Detroit whose lyrics explored the supernatural and horror in a genre called "horrorcore."

Peterson found references in their belongings to a song by a rap group called Boondox. In the song "Seven" the lyrics mimic the child's rhyme "A tisket, a tasket," followed by a reference to "the scarecrow's out his casket." It advised people to turn out their lights and lock their doors and pray that the scarecrow passed them by.

The scarecrow had stopped at Susan's door.

Merrilee had called Paul her "scarecrow god," Peterson remembered.

He also found references to something called Magic: The Gathering. It seemed to be a combination of mysticism, role-playing and a card game. Those who played were "Planeswalkers" and traveled between universes.

They had been part of an anime club at school. A male teacher sponsored the club, and he was not very cooperative when the detectives asked him about the activities club members participated in. Anime is a style of cartoons that have mostly Japanese characters. The cartoons that are frequently shown in daytime are harmless and younger children watch them. At night, the cartoons turn dark.

The searches of the house had turned up plays that Jennifer had written and the teens had acted out. The plays were strange and full of fantasy. Jennifer's name in the plays was Lilly.

He had found books in David's room containing Celtic myths and legends. There was a book called *Full Contact Magick: A Book of Shadows for the Wiccan Warrior*. There were tomes about vampirism—about drinking blood. David was displaying in his reading habits the same fascination with dark themes as his sister and her boyfriend, he thought. All four teens had convinced themselves and each other that they had been together in lives past and that they needed to do certain things to continue to be together in future lives. The books talked about stalking people in the night, cutting their throats and drinking from their open wounds.

They are sick little monkeys, Peterson thought.

Peterson lived in Cleburne, at best an hour's drive from his job in Roanoke. He worked long hours on the case. Sometimes it seemed like he had just arrived home when it was time to get in his truck and make the return trip. Sometimes he spent entire weekends poring over the case. He found a decent, inexpensive motel near Roanoke and spent many nights and weekends there as the case progressed. He stayed at his own expense. It seemed to be the only way he could get any rest, though it wasn't good for his marriage— he knew that. But Ivy, his wife, was patient. She knew what a dedicated officer he was, and she knew he was obsessed with making an airtight case against the teens.

Sometimes, even with the help of a number of other officers, the enormity of the investigation almost over-whelmed the detective.

It's like eating an elephant, he had to keep reminding himself. *You take one bite at a time.*

Finally, word came from the scientific tests performed on the evidence taken from the house. The frayed wires at the end of the extension cord that had been set up to elec-trocute Susan had DNA on them. The DNA belonged to Paul Henson Jr. Paul said he was not in the house and had not been part of the conspiracy, yet one of the fingerprints on a blood-smeared wall was his. The fingerprint and the DNA on the frayed cord showed that he had been there after Susan shed blood, and that he was the one who devised that possible killing weapon.

Kate's Journal

Wednesday, October 8, 2008

My birthday! Sheryl tells me Susan came to see her last night.
Says she is OK—not to worry. Sheryl is crying.

24

The Texas Memorial

The Mortens continued to clean out Susan's house. There was so much to do and they wanted to go home. They made more trips to the Dumpster, threw away everything in the refrigerator, and packed the unopened foodstuffs from the cabinets and took them to a community food center for the poor. And the cleaning continued.

The press showed up and camped out in the driveway. A reporter from the local CBS affiliate asked for an interview. Kate didn't want to do it. But the reporter promised to keep the interview short. She just wanted to have something good to say about Susan from the family, she said. Kate reluctantly agreed.

Then a reporter from the local FOX channel demanded an interview too. Kate became very upset. No more. She just could not do any more interviews. She locked the front door and refused to answer repeated doorbell rings. The news crews stayed in the driveway past ten P.M.

Reporters did find neighbors who were willing to talk. One woman told a reporter from the *Dallas Morning News* that Susan was "caring and witty." The neighbor said that Jennifer rode her bicycle to work and that she had run away several times. Another neighbor told the reporter that the family kept to themselves most of the time but that he did know that Susan had not approved of her daughter's boyfriend. But he'd had no idea that the situation had become violent.

The memorial service was slated for seven P.M. on Thursday, October 9, 2008. Kate and Stephen drove to the jail in Denton that afternoon and asked to visit with their granddaughter Jennifer, but learned that visitation hours were from seven to nine P.M. that night. They would be at Susan's memorial service then and would not be allowed to see Jennifer any other time. There was no visitation for juvenile offenders as young as David that day, so they went back to the house at The Parks of Roanoke and continued to work.

Kate was looking for pictures of Susan to display at the memorial service. Kate and Stephen found some they liked and also found a memory book their daughter had made. Susan's neighbor, Sheryl Barnes, picked the Mortens up for the ride to the memorial service. It had been only a few days earlier, Sheryl told them, that she had stopped by a garage sale Susan was holding to show off her new Mercedes convertible, and Susan had been excited to go for a ride in it as soon as possible, her neighbor said.

Now there was only a box with Susan's ashes inside. This was not the convertible ride Sheryl had thought to give her friend.

The church was in a strip mall. Kate was amazed at such a thing, but inside it was nice, she thought. Sheryl had bought pink roses for Susan. They had been her favorite.

Detectives Brian Peterson and Chris Almonrode attended. Kate was grateful for their kindness. A number of Susan's work friends came, and they spoke of happy memories of her kindness, her humor and the impact she'd had on their lives. About fifty people were there. Susan had made a lot of friends during her time in Texas.

The Mortens were up early again the next morning. Their daughter and son-in-law left with a loaded U-Haul trailer. Kate wandered around the house, touching Susan's things that were left and picking up a few more items to take back to Minnesota. It was time to leave. She didn't expect to ever be there again. She placed flowers and photographs on the blood spot in front of Jennifer's door and she and Stephen slowly walked to their loaded van and drove away.

They left the children's rooms. There was nothing in either of them they wanted or could even bear to look at. They had learned from the detectives that Jennifer now had asked for a lawyer and refused to talk about the murder. By this time most young people are crying, scared and sorry, Peterson said. Jennifer had shown no sign of guilt or emotion. Certainly no remorse.

Sheryl and another neighbor, Kim Aiken, had promised the Mortens that they would deal with whatever was left in the house. They packed everything and called a charity, which picked everything up and took it away. The two women found a few things they believed that Kate had missed and would like to have. She had told them she would be back for the trials, so they stored the treasures for her.

On the Mortens' drive home, Richard Bailey called. Kate didn't want to talk to him, but she listened to what he had to say. He had heard the Mortens were in town. He was on his way to visit Jennifer. He said he would call back after he saw her. Kate just wanted off the telephone. She could hardly bear to hear his voice.

He called after his visit and reported that Jennifer said she'd cried herself to sleep the night before.

"It's about time she showed some emotion," Kate retorted. "Is she sorry about what she did or just sorry for herself?"

They didn't talk about bad things, Richard told her. They talked about what they would do when she was able to come home.

"I'm going to get my kids," he said.

Kate exploded. "They are never coming home!"

An argument ensued. Kate asked him how much Richard knew about what had happened. Nothing, he said. He didn't want to know. He was going to testify for his children, and knowing what happened might taint that testimony.

Kate was angry and shouting. She wanted him to know how bad it had been, but he insisted that she should not tell him.

"They stabbed her in the stomach and then the back of the neck and then they slit her throat," she yelled. "After she was dead and to make sure she was dead they continued to stab her in the neck!"

She could hear nothing on the other end of the connection. She believed he had placed his phone on "mute."

He came back on the line.

"I don't want to hear," he said.

"They ambushed her in Jennifer's doorway!"

"Have a good day," Richard said, and ended the connection.

Kate sat crying as the car rolled on toward Oklahoma City, destination: Minnesota. Her former son-in-law seemed to think they were all still one happy family. She and Stephen had left Denton without trying to see either of their grandchildren again. They just couldn't bear it.

25

Reports from Friends

Several Roanoke officers went to Northwest High School looking for friends of all three of the teens. They conducted interviews and learned several things that hadn't come out before. Texas Ranger Tracy Murphree compiled the reports into his master report of the case.

The officers contacted one girl whose name had been on several notes to and from Paul that were found in his bedroom. The girl had asked if she could go to Canada too, and Paul had replied that he would have to ask the others. Then he wrote that she could come along; meanwhile, she should get together as much cash as she could and things that could be pawned to pay for the trip. He wrote that they were leaving on Tuesday, September 23, and that she should meet them in front of the Walmart store in Roanoke.

The girl decided not to go. She talked to Paul on Tuesday

to let him know. He replied that there had been a postpone-
ment anyway, because he was ill.

A male teen told the officers that he had become friends
with Paul at the beginning of the school year. About three
weeks earlier, he said, Paul had become more aggressive at
school. He talked a lot about becoming a vampire, the boy
said. Paul told him that he believed in reincarnation and
that he was certain that he'd previously been an executioner
in the 1800s. At one point he told the other boy that he
was going to get his dad's gun and go to Denton "to take
care of some business."

Another of Paul's friends told the officers that Paul had
become increasingly more aggressive in the past few weeks.
He was confrontational and threatening, the boy said.

A girl told the officers that Paul was a practicing Wiccan.
Jennifer also practiced the Wiccan witchcraft, she said, and
she and Jennifer had performed Wiccan rituals, including
meditation and looking back into past lives. Paul was active
in role-playing games, she said.

Jennifer had talked to one friend about Paul's relationship with Merrilee. The girl said she asked Jennifer about
a week before the murder how everything was going, and
Jennifer had replied, "Everything is going as planned."

Another girl talked about Paul's split personality. He
had two personalities, she said. One was mild and the other
was violent. Paul and both Jennifer and Merrilee had sex
together, she said.

Yet another girl also admitted to knowing that the three
teens were having a "threesome" sexual relationship. Paul was

strange, the girl said. He had severe mood swings and at times he would mumble and chant in an "unknown language."

One teenage girl told investigators more about Paul's other personality, the one she thought was named "Thomas," and who she said once told her "Paul is going to kill if I let him out." (Murphree and Peterson had learned that the boy actually called his second personality "Talos," and they believed that "Talos" was the violent one, but perhaps this girl had her names and her personalities crossed.)

She knew Jennifer too, the girl said.

"Jennifer loves to hate her mother."

The officers found a girl who said that she had been involved in a sexual relationship with Merrilee before she took up with Jennifer and Paul. Those two, she said, were too involved in the game of Dungeons & Dragons and had made the game a reality.

One of the students pulled out of class that Monday by Roanoke police was a girl named Harley Greco. She had not known about the murder, and she was horrified to learn that her friend Jennifer had been a part of it. Jennifer was sweet and happy and funny, Harley said. She wasn't a killer, Harley was sure of it.

Many of the teens were not surprised to learn that Paul had been involved in murder. There was just something about him. . . . There were several officers at the school, Harley remembered years later, and vans carrying television reporters outside. The reporters were kept off the school grounds and she avoided them going home. The story was on all the television channels that night. It was all the kids at Northwest High School could talk about for several days.

Then life intervened, and young couples broke up and others fell in love and tests were scheduled and normalcy returned.

"We talked about it nonstop for a couple of weeks, and then we got back to our lives and forgot about it."

Both Harley and Paul belonged to a group of kids who thought of themselves as outcasts, and they hung together. She first got to know Paul from Anime Club, and she met Jennifer later after Paul began dating her. They had lunch together, usually in the library where their favorite counselor had an office, and sometimes they got together after school. The school officials referred to that counselor's students as "troubled," she said, and they knew they could talk to the special counselor at almost any time. Harley said she was considered an outcast because she was new. Her parents had divorced and she wound up in the school district living with her father after the school year had already begun and cliques had been formed. She was upset at the abrupt change in her life. She wore dark clothing in the goth-style, and she sometimes became upset during class. The outcasts were her friends, she said.

Harley was a sophomore the year that Paul was a junior. Paul was dark—odd, she thought. He had long, curly dark brown hair and he wore dark clothing. Anime is a name for Japanese cartoons often shown on cable. During the daytime, the cartoons can be light and funny, and younger children like them. At night the cartoons turn darker, and it was these cartoons that the members of the club watched and talked about in their weekly meetings. The cartoon characters are mostly Japanese and the cartoons take place in Japan or in fictional countries. Some are about everyday life. Others are about demons. The club members were fascinated by them and enjoyed getting together for their weekly chats. The subject matter when the club members met sometimes veered off from the television shows. Harley recalled one day when Paul began talking about himself. He believed in reincarnation. He bragged about his past life as an executioner to British royalty. He was sure this had happened. He described things that he had done in detail.

"We all talked about weird things, but this was the weirdest," Harley said.

Paul had some strange habits. Sometimes he would cut a finger and suck the blood from the cut. She considered his friends to be weird as well. They were a little intimidating.

"He was easygoing, but he had a temper. Sometimes he punched walls."

Harley knew Merrilee but had no idea that Paul was dating her. She only saw him around school with Jennifer. But Jennifer wasn't really a member of this group of kids. She didn't wear dark clothing. Jennifer wore bright, pretty clothes, and she was beautiful, with shiny blonde hair, Harley remembers. She always seemed happy and easygoing. After Jennifer and Paul began dating, Harley became friends with her. Jennifer spent a lot of time at Harley's house in Rhome, Texas, another small town in the huge school district. But Harley never went to Jennifer's house. They liked to listen to music and talk about school and boys. They never talked about reincarnation or any of Paul's other interests. She never heard Jennifer talk about playing the game of Dungeons & Dragons. She seemed normal and happy. They had divorced parents in common, but Jennifer didn't talk about that much. She never talked much about her family, and Harley had not even known that she had a little brother. Harley thought she was a normal teenage girl, much like herself.

"I never saw it coming with her. We all knew that her mother didn't like Paul. But then again, he was not somebody I would bring home to my parents."

The two did listen to emo bands together. Harley remembers listening to songs by bands like My Chemical Romance and Fall Out Boy. She described emo as "people wearing dark clothes, being cutters. Emo was a really bad, cheap imitation of goth."

After the teens were arrested in South Dakota and returned to Denton County, another friend of the girls visited Jennifer in the Denton County Jail, Harley said. That girl came back with a story Jennifer told her.

"She said she was the first one to pick up the baseball bat."

It had made a certain amount of sense to imagine Paul carrying out a murder plan. And he had been absent from school that Thursday and Friday. But not Jennifer, Harley said. She just was not like that. "We all thought Paul did it. She just couldn't have done anything. I still want to say it was Paul's idea."

Harley and Jennifer had often texted and talked on their cell phones. On Saturday, September 27, Harley's phone rang. It was Jennifer.

"Where are you?" Harley had asked her.

On a family trip, Jennifer replied. She wasn't sure when she would be home. Harley recalled absolutely no sign from her friend of what she had really been up to.

After interviewing the students, a Roanoke detective drove to Hurst to interview some of Susan Bailey's coworkers. One woman said that she and Susan had become friends. Susan was worried about her son, David, she'd told the friend. He was fighting a lot and was getting worse. Susan said she might send him to military school.

Susan also had confided about her daughter. Jennifer had always been such a sweet child. Then she started dating a really weird boy and now she was hateful, hostile and disobedient. She caught her in lies, Susan confided. She just didn't know what to do with the girl.

On the day of the murder, Susan had been upset and in a hurry to get home. She could not reach Jennifer by telephone, she told the friend, and she was worried about her daughter.

Susan did not like Paul and she had tried, without success, to make Jennifer stop seeing him, according to another coworker. She also said that Susan had told her how much Jennifer had changed since she'd started dating him, and Susan didn't like the change.

The coworkers said that Susan hoped that going to the art college would take her daughter's mind off the boyfriend.

Kate wrote in her journal on October 18, 2008, that she and Stephen were getting ready to drive to Arizona for the winter. She had organized all the things they had brought home from Susan's house in the garage and moved some things, like her sewing machine, into the house. She was taking a few things to Arizona, but not many, she said. Everyone who had gone to Texas now had bronchitis, she wrote. They believed they were having breathing difficulties because of the cat and dog hair in the house and because of the blood spores in the air.

They arrived at their winter home and settled in. Kate wrote on November 11, 2008, that she had finally drafted a letter to Jennifer. She had decided the right thing to do was to correspond with her granddaughter, and she planned to write to her once a week.

"It's not a real nice one," she wrote in her journal. "But not real bad either. Inserted an envelope with stamp. We'll see if she writes."

She did. Jennifer replied from the Denton County Jail. She wrote that she missed her grandparents. She had waited to write, she said, because she didn't want to write something stupid and wanted to think about what to say. She hoped that someday Kate would forgive her. Jennifer wrote that she had found God. She relied on her faith to get her through the days, she said. She realized that she had lost everything and owned nothing in this world anymore. All she had was God, she said.

Jennifer asked her grandmother to send her photographs of David and her mother. Oh, and by the way, her father wondered whether Kate would send him Susan's pearl ring and necklace. They had been his mother's, she said.

Jennifer wrote that she was praying that her grandmother would find peace one day.

Kate's Journal

Tuesday, February 3, 2009

Been writing with Jennifer. Got a nasty letter from her today. Couldn't sleep all night. She's calling me Kate, am insensitive to her feelings & she doesn't want to be puppeted like her cousins. If I can't abide by her wishes GOD BE WITH ME—swear? Could be go to hell. Wrote back but waiting a few days to mail it.

26

Murphree's Investigation

Texas Ranger Tracy Murphree was a sports fan. He attended nearly all the home games of the Texas Rangers baseball team and he was a staunch Dallas Cowboys football fan. In his office at the headquarters of the Texas Department of Public Safety in Denton he had two large pictures. Over his right shoulder was a big picture of the great Cowboys coach Tom Landry (Murphree had never forgiven Jerry Jones for firing Landry after he bought the team), and over his left shoulder hung a picture of Ronald Reagan, in Murphree's opinion one of the greatest presidents who ever lived.

Murphree was a handsome man but he suffered from early male pattern baldness so, like many men, he figured his best recourse was to shave his head. He rarely was seen without his signature Stetson hat or a baseball cap. Some joked that he must sleep in them. He had a beautiful blonde wife and four children. Murphree was a religious man, a passionate patriot and a devout Texan to the core. He was liked, respected and admired throughout the state family of law enforcement officers. Murphree always had wanted to be a Texas Ranger, and with his family and numerous friends, he was a happy man.

On October 15, he prepared affidavits for search warrants for all the seized computers and thumb drives and for the cell phones that had been in the bathtub. Then they were taken to a lab for analysis.

He got the results of the tests on the two knives found in the backyard. They had no blood or DNA on them. They had been outdoors quite a while. He believed the teens had practiced throwing the knives as part of one of their fantasy role-playing games. The chocolate pudding that had sat around the house for several days after Susan refused to eat it had contained a big dose of crushed over-the-counter medicine. One of the bloody fingerprints they cut out of the hallway walls had been determined to be from Paul.

He sat behind his desk one day early in the investigation and thought about the whole picture. And he came to some conclusions. He believed that Jennifer was the mastermind of the plot. She was the one who really wanted her mother dead. David had been in on the plan from the beginning, Murphree believed. He and his sister were very close. He was part of the poisoned-pudding episode. He had helped stab his mother. He had laughed about her death in the squad car on the way back to Texas. He was very young, but he was not innocent.

Murphree did not believe that Jennifer ever, not for a

minute, believed in the "Talos" personality that Paul liked to flaunt. Jennifer used sex and the fantasy life that Paul loved to manipulate him, the Ranger thought.

She was a weird kid, Murphree thought. *She found ol' Paul and used him.*

He remembered a short interview with Jennifer after she was ensconced in a jail cell in the adult section of the Denton County Jail. She had played the innocent young girl, talking in a small, childish voice. She professed that she was not involved in the death of her mother.

"I know about Merrilee," he told her.

Murphree remembered what happened next with a shudder.

"Fucking evil came out on her face," he recalls. "She realized that Merrilee had broken the pact. If she could have come across that table and killed me, she would have."

Merrilee White was also a pawn, he decided. The other two told the younger girl what to do, but they didn't let her in on all of their plans.

She was so afraid they were going to leave her behind that she tried to stab her mother.

Merrilee White had "lawyered up" and wasn't saying anything to Fort Worth police. Her parents had bailed her out of the detention center. Her mother, Amy, was in full protective mode and continued now to deny that the girl ever had any intentions of hurting her that morning when she stood over her with a butcher knife raised over her head. Murphree, Investigator Larry Kish and Detective Brian Peterson met with the mother to explain things.

Merrilee was part of a conspiracy to murder and could

be charged with capital murder, they said. Her age took the death penalty off the table. No one under the age of eighteen could be put to death in Texas. But it was obvious that Merrilee had conspired with the others to kill their parents. Her mother couldn't protect her from those charges. David Bailey was younger than Merrilee and he was facing a long prison term. That could also be Merrilee's fate if she didn't cooperate. They wanted her to tell them everything she knew about the other three. They wanted to know about the pact to kill and to keep quiet no matter what. They wanted to know about the dynamics among the two girls and Paul. They wanted to know about the fantasy games, the sex, the music and the role playing. She had to tell them about the scarecrow, they said.

Amy White didn't want her daughter to talk to them. But she didn't want her in prison either. So Merrilee and her lawyer met with the detectives and the Denton County prosecutor.

Merrilee told them that she knew Paul first and fell in love with him. Then he introduced her to Jennifer and the three of them started hanging out. She talked about the three-way sex and the relationship she had with "Talos," Paul's claimed second personality. He had been an executioner in a prior life, she explained. They did a lot of role-playing games and acted out some plays that Jennifer wrote. And they made a plan to kill their parents. That wasn't role playing, she said. It was really going to happen. She had been there when Jennifer ground up the drugs and made the chocolate pudding. Maybe it would kill Susan. Maybe it would put her to sleep and they could put her in the bathtub and electrocute her. They weren't sure, but they had plenty of other ideas if that didn't work. Paul was going to shoot his dad and stepmother that Monday night before Merrilee was arrested the next morning. (She later found out that they hadn't come home from work that night, and Paul took the gun and went back to Jennifer's house.) Merrilee was going to stab her mother, and they all were going to blitz Susan and stab her to death. Then they were all going to go together to Canada and live happily ever after. Merrilee was fuzzy about what was supposed to happen after they crossed the border. She supposed they would get jobs and all live together. She just knew that she was supposed to go with them and was prevented from doing so by her mother. They had made a pact. None of them would ever rat out the others, and if need be, they would all go down together. She was distraught that she had to break that pact. But she didn't want to go to prison for the rest of her life.

Because of that interview, no Denton County charges were filed against Merrilee, though she still faced charges in the attack on her mother in Tarrant County. Even though Amy White wanted her daughter out of trouble, Fort Worth police were not willing to drop the charges. After months of negotiations, Merrilee eventually pleaded "true" to aggravated assault in juvenile court and was assessed five years of probation. Her mother moved her to another school district, where the fantasy life she lived with Jennifer and Paul began to recede. Few people even knew that Merrilee had been part of the conspiracy to kill Susan. Because of her juvenile status and perhaps because she lived in a different city and county, her attack on her mother was not publicized. In her journal, Kate Morten wrote that Merrilee got off easy.

In March 2009, Denton County Sheriff's Investigator Don Britt contacted Murphree. Britt was one of the detectives who'd looked for runaway Paul Henson Jr. at the Bailey house back before Susan's murder. He had recently interviewed another female inmate on an unconnected case, he said. That woman was a cellmate to Jennifer. The woman told Britt that Jennifer had talked to her about the murder and had told the woman that she and Paul were having sex when Susan walked in on them. Paul began stabbing her, Jennifer said. He kept stabbing until he thought she was dead. But Susan started moving, Jennifer told the cellmate, but she didn't want her mother to suffer so she "finished her off." She said David was in his room the whole time. When he walked out of his room and found his mother dead in the hallway, he fainted, she said.

Murphree listened to Jennifer's latest story with skepticism. The facts didn't conform with that tale, he thought. Both Jennifer and David had participated, and Jennifer's stab wounds were inflicted before her mother was down on the floor.

Detective Britt recalled walking through the jail shortly after Jennifer's initial arrest and seeing her sitting in a holding cell. He'd looked long and hard at her. She was a liar and a killer. He now knew the whole story. She had been harboring Paul when he was in the house, but Britt had not had enough probable cause to search without permission. Now Susan Bailey was dead. Jennifer looked up briefly, but when she realized who Britt was, she quickly lowered her head again. Britt walked on. How could those children have killed their mother? Could he have done more? Had he known what was to come, he would have found Paul and dragged him out of whatever hidey-hole he had slithered into. But hindsight wasn't much help now, and at least the killers were in custody. Still, Britt couldn't forget the victim and her assurances that no one was in her home except the people who belonged there.

She was so wrong, he thought, *and it had cost her her life.*

Kate's Journal

Friday, March 20, 2009

Having a hard time in Susan's house. Want to touch every-thing she had her hands on. Could feel her there. Cried a lot.

27

Back in Texas

On March 14, 2009, the Mortens began another drive to Roanoke, Texas. Detective Brian Peterson had called to tell them that the prosecutors assigned to the case wanted to walk through the house to reconstruct the crime. Kate wasn't sure if the keys would still work at the house. But they made the drive and were able to enter. The electricity was off, but apparently the house had not gone into foreclosure yet.

They met with Peterson and Assistant District Attorneys Allison Sartain and Victoria Abbott at two P.M. the next day. Kate wrote in her journal that she learned that Paul Henson Jr. was in a psychiatric hospital with stress-related issues. They needed him to be in better mental health before trying him as an adult.

Kate noticed that Peterson was having a hard time going upstairs. It brought back memories of the awful things he saw that Sunday morning when he had to look at Susan lying there in her own drying blood from so many cuts made by her own children. It made Kate sad. But eventually everyone climbed the stairs. They tried to recreate the scene from what they knew. They told her again about the books in David's room on cults, devil worship and mysticism.

The prosecutors wanted to see Jennifer's letters to Kate. And they wanted the Mortens to visit David to try to get him to talk about what happened.

The Mortens spent the morning of March 20, 2009, back in Susan's house. They gathered a few more mementoes and then checked out of their hotel. Then they drove to Denton. They were going to visit David.

They didn't have an appointment but were told they could have five minutes with him. Kate wrote in her journal that he came out smiling and hugged her. She was crying and he was saying, "It's okay, Grandma. It's okay."

"I said, it is NOT OKAY, David, and what happened? He said he couldn't talk about it and just wanted to be happy. It made me angry. I wanted him to say he was sorry and he didn't."

28

Plea Bargains

Trying juveniles is very different than working on adult cases. Juvenile law is considered civil law, not criminal law. Juveniles are not "defendants," but "respondents." They are not "indicted," they are issued a "petition." The question isn't guilty or not guilty, but true or not true. A true finding is put into a document that is served not only on the young person but on the parents. A sentence is not called "punishment" but "disposition." The theory on juvenile crime is that the cases need to be moved quickly through the system so rehabilitation can begin as soon as possible. The idea is to rehabilitate the juvenile, not punish him.

Time passed slowly in the Denton County Jail. The teens would remain there until their cases were adjudicated and they had been assessed sentences. The investigators continued to amass evidence for trials, and all three of the teens were assigned court-appointed lawyers. County taxpayers would bear the expense of the defense of each of them.

Victoria Abbott was chief of juvenile crimes, and she took the job of prosecuting Paul and David. Because all three cases involved the same evidence, she also did most of the work on Jennifer's case as well, working with adult prosecutor Mary Miller, who had been assigned the case.

Abbott had been with Denton County for about a year. Before that she'd served in the public defender's office in Dallas County, working as a defense attorney specializing in juvenile cases, and before that she worked in the Dallas County District Attorney's Office with such legendary district attorneys as Henry Wade and John Vance. She had been working with juvenile offenders since 1989. She had prosecuted a great deal of juvenile crime. This was not her first case involving teens who had killed their parents. But those other juveniles had shot their parents, and sometimes youngsters who fire guns are not really cognizant of what happens next. Not really. They pull the trigger in anger or bravado and only later realize the finality of death. Stabbing someone is very different. Stabbing is up close and very personal. It's messy, brutal and bloody. Blood spurts from wounds and sluices over everything and everyone nearby. The stabber's hands get slick with blood. It gets all over them and then it turns sticky. In this case there were twenty-six separate wounds. *Twenty-six*. And Susan had been practically beheaded. It had been relatively slow. She knew she was dying. They knew she was dying. They saw the gaping wounds. Yet they did not stop. It was an awful crime.

The juvenile justice system is not meant to attach a

stigma to those who pass through it. That is the reason that juvenile cases are protected from public eye. Every effort is made for the child to be released on bail until trial. When a juvenile turns eighteen he usually starts over with a clean slate. No public record. But not in all cases. Some cases are so serious, the conduct has been so violent, the "child" is considered so dangerous that they are held without bond. Jennifer was an adult and considered a flight risk. She was held without bail. Paul and David, both juveniles at the time of the crime, also were held without bond.

Older juveniles can be certified as adults. Because of age, the nature of the crime or other circumstances, a juvenile can be found eligible to be tried as a legal adult. At that time he is moved to the adult judicial system with its harsher terms, its public proceedings and its possible longer punishments.

The prosecutors decided this was the proper adjudication for Paul, and they went to work on the process. He stayed in juvenile detention until the hearing that pronounced him a legal adult. Then he was moved to the adult section of the Denton County Jail. He was indicted for capital murder and would be tried as an adult.

As for David, that sweet-faced cherubic boy, the officers and prosecutors were convinced that he was part of the conspiracy and had participated in the murder. He was too young to certify as an adult, but there was another option. That option was called a "determinate" sentence, which could be as long as forty years. David would be tried as a juvenile. On his eighteenth birthday, there would be a hearing before a judge. Evidence would be presented as to his culpability in the crime and his conduct in the interim. A judge would then decide whether he would be transferred to adult prison to finish his sentence. A juvenile not given a determinate sentence can only be detained until his nineteenth birthday.

Juveniles can be, and usually are, released on bail until their trials. But in this case there was really no one to whom they could release David. His mother was dead and his maternal grandparents were certainly not going to raise him. Though Richard was upset when his children were arrested, he did not obtain custody or bail them out of jail. And David also was considered a flight risk, so his chances of having bail set were not good.

David stayed in juvenile hall. Every ten days after a juvenile is detained, there must be a hearing to determine whether the juvenile should be released. His hearings went on and on, but the judge never allowed him to go free on bail.

Victoria Abbott worked closely with Tracy Murphree, Larry Kish and Brian Peterson. She was impressed by the investigators' hard work and the evidence they'd compiled. They had made a good case should it need to go to trial, she believed. The officers went above and beyond their duty on this case, she said.

Some parts of the evidence Abbott saw were horrifying beyond their face value. The officers brought her the video from the Walmart store from that Thursday afternoon when David could be seen buying the cleaner. There was something awful about a small boy pedaling his bicycle to a store for cleaning supplies because he planned to kill his mother that night and knew it would be bloody. But they also brought her a video from a few nights earlier at the same store. Susan had brought her children to the store to shop. While she searched the shelves for bread and milk, Jennifer and David held hands and skipped down the aisles. Knowing that they knew what they were about to do, the prosecutor felt a chill at this behavior.

The older teens wrote plays and acted them out, she learned. Jennifer usually starred in the plays. Her character name was Lilly, and Abbott wondered whether the name had any significance.

Abbott's trip to the house was another chilling event. It was one thing to look dispassionately at crime-scene photos and count the wounds on the body and try to place in your mind's eye where each room was located. It was quite another to walk up those stairs that Susan had trod that night, unaware of the horror that awaited her at the top; to look into the game room and the bathrooms and to step around the spot on the hallway floor where the carpet had been ripped up and the bloodstains covered over. To smell the lingering odor of blood and death. That was a moment when you could almost hear Susan's screams and imagine her begging her daughter to call 911 and to hear Jennifer's reply of "no." That was the part that made the prosecutor determined to do her best to achieve justice for Susan. That was the part that made it hard to go to sleep at night.

TRUE BILL OF INDICTMENT

In the name and by authority of the state of Texas

The GRAND JURORS, in and for the County of Denton, State of Texas, duly organized, impaneled, and sworn as such, at the July Term, A.D., 2009, of the District Court of the 367th Judicial District in and for said county and state, upon their oaths, present in and to said Court that JENNIFER BAILEY, who is hereinafter styled defendant, on or about the 25th day of September, 2008, and anterior to the presentment of this indictment, in the county and state aforesaid, did then and there intentionally cause the death of an individual, namely, Susan Bailey, by stabbing and/or cutting and/or slashing Susan with a deadly weapon, to-wit: a knife and/or a sharp instrument the exact nature and description which is unknown to the Grand Jury, and the defendant was then and there in the course of committing or attempting to commit the offense of robbery of Susan Bailey;

against the peace and dignity of the state.

(signed) PAUL JOHNSON
Criminal District Attorney of Denton County, Texas

(signed by the foreman of the grand jury)

29

Capital Murder

On December 11, 2008, a grand jury had issued indictments for capital murder for Jennifer Bailey and Paul Henson Jr. and declared David Bailey a child in need of supervision, which is the state's description of a juvenile offender. Capital murder in Texas carries the penalty of death or life in prison. Because none of them had been eighteen when the crime was committed, the death penalty could not be assessed to any of them. But they could be sent to prison for life without parole. And life behind bars looms large to someone not yet even in their twenties.

In Texas, an indictment for capital murder can be assessed if murder is committed in the act of committing another crime, like a person being killed while being robbed. It also could apply if a police officer or firefighter had been murdered in the line of duty, if more than one victim was involved in the same crime spree or if a child under the age of six had been killed. In this case, the teens had taken Susan's bank card and attempted to use it. They also had taken her car. Because Victoria Abbott and the other prosecutors were seeking a determinate sentence for David, the grand jury also heard his case. Grand jurors agreed that a determinate sentence was proper for David. He would not be released—at least not without a judge's order—when he reached legal adulthood. He would be transferred from a juvenile facility to a unit of the Texas Department of Criminal Justice.

Had the murder occurred three years earlier, both Jennifer and Paul could have been subject to the death penalty. The Supreme Court had ruled in 1989 that sixteen- and seventeen-year-old offenders could be executed, and it wasn't until March 2005 that the Supreme Court issued a new ruling stating that executing anyone under the age of eighteen was "cruel and unusual punishment."

At that time the court reported that there was a national consensus against putting juveniles to death, stating that teenagers are too immature to be held accountable for their actions to the extent of being put to death as punishment for them. The decision also was influenced by a desire to bring the United States more in line with international practice. The United States was the only country that executed people younger than eighteen years of age.

That decision cancelled the executions of seventy-three people on death rows around the country who'd been under the age of eighteen when they'd committed capital crimes. Twenty-three of those were in Texas.

Justice Anthony M. Kennedy wrote the court's opinion: "From a moral standpoint, it would be misguided to equate the failings of a minor with those of an adult, for a greater possibility exists that a minor's character deficiencies will be reformed," Kennedy wrote. The Supreme Court ruling thus saved Jennifer and Paul from the possibility of execution. But the ruling did not preclude them from life without parole. Both teens wanted something to look forward to sometime in their lives and agreed to plea bargains. But before Paul could enter a plea agreement, he had to be declared a legal adult. Sheriff's Investigator Jeff Coats attended the hearing along with Ranger Tracy Murphree, Detective Brian Peterson and Investigator Larry Kish. Paul was sitting on a backseat in the courtroom with a detention officer sitting beside him. In his peripheral vision, Coats could see that Paul was raising his hands to his head and seemed to be fiddling with something. When he was called to the front of the courtroom to be admonished by the judge, he passed by Coats and the officer could see his head. Paul had been twisting his hair into two points. As he stood before the judge, Paul appeared to have devil's horns coming from his head. Coats was astonished, but the judge apparently didn't notice.

Coats believed that Paul's father, Paul Henson Sr., never could fathom the fact that his life had truly been in danger at the hands of his son. As Coats took charge of the boy, now legally a man, he noticed that Paul Jr. held a blank stare as though he had no idea where he was and what was happening. As Coats started to escort him to his new home in the adult portion of the county lockup, Paul Henson Sr. followed them to the courtroom door.

"I love you, son!" he yelled, as Paul disappeared from sight.

Coats thought about the evidence that pointed to Paul's intent to shoot his father and stepmother to death. Only their happenstance decision to have dinner and see a movie before coming home that night saved their lives, Coats believed. He could not understand how Paul Sr. could still support him. But he knew that parental love is strong, and it sometimes allows parents to turn a blind eye to their children's actions.

On June 9, 2009, Paul Henson Jr. formally accepted a plea bargain. He submitted a handwritten confession and pled guilty to a reduced charge of murder in return for a sixty-year sentence. His release date is September 26, 2068, but he can become eligible for parole on September 26, 2038. He will be fifty-seven years old if he is released at his first opportunity for parole, but there is no assurance that will happen. The Texas Board of Pardons and Paroles will hear his case at that time and make a decision based on his actions while in prison and input from the public, including the law enforcement officers who worked the case, before allowing him to walk free. The board will consider the particulars of the crime in its decision. Murphree and Peterson both have indicated they will stand before the board to ask members not to release any of the teens before their sentences are fully carried out. It is not likely that Paul or Jennifer will be released before that time.

Kate Morten wrote in her journal that, in his confession, Paul said that he and Jennifer made David stab his mother after she was dead. That may have been true. The wounds attributed to David were superficial. No matter. Legally David participated in the conspiracy and in the crime.

Paul's decision to plea bargain was a lucky one. A capital murder conviction by a jury likely would have carried a penalty of life without parole. Jurors likely would have been horrified at the brutality the teens showed, and a "no parole" option would have been open to them. Paul avoided that by entering the plea agreement. When his "good time" and his calendar time actually served add up to thirty years, he can have the parole hearing. In Texas, inmates in certain classifications can earn "good time," i.e. good conduct, in prison by taking jobs in their units or taking educational courses or even tutoring other inmates. Depending on their classification (and their classification depends on their conduct) they earn different amounts of good time, but the most that can be earned is thirty days of good time added to thirty days of real time.

After Paul entered his plea and was sentenced, prosecutors asked Murphree to interview him. Paul had nothing to lose or gain now, and he might be willing to talk more about what happened that night. Neither Jennifer nor David had been adjudicated, and prosecutors wanted all the ammunition they could find in the event their cases went to trial. It was worth a shot.

A few days later Murphree talked to Paul in an interview room in the Denton County Jail. He told the teen, *You've pled and you'll soon be going down to prison. Nothing more can happen to you legally. So now I'd like to hear your side of the story.*

Paul's eyes rolled back in his head and he underwent a transformation of sorts right before Murphree's eyes. He was becoming "Talos," the Ranger realized.

"Don't you start that shit with me," he thundered at Paul. "That's not real and I know it. Did you know that Jennifer blamed it all on you?"

The "transformation" stopped. Paul sat up and began to act like a normal kid. He agreed to tell Murphree what had actually happened.

What people think of as split or multiple personalities is known by professionals as dissociative identity disorder. It is real. Whether it was real for Paul or simply an attention-getting pose had not been decided when he was arrested, though the officers suspected the latter. And whether he was officially diagnosed while in prison is not public record. But some things Murphree knew. Dissociation is a coping mechanism. There is much that is not known about the controversial findings of researchers, but most believe the problems begin in early childhood and can be associated with emotional or mental neglect or abuse even when nothing physical has occurred. When abuse is suffered, some children dissociate themselves from what is happening to them. They somehow ignore the abuse they cannot consciously tolerate and assign it to another part of their personality to deal with. So they develop a separate personality that undergoes the abuse instead of their own personality. It gives them a scapegoat who handles the suffering for them.

According to authorities, the disorder is characterized by two or more distinct identities that have power over the person's behavior. People who have the disorder but have not been treated do not remember what happens when an alternate personality takes over.

This did not seem to be the case for Paul. He seemed to

know all about his alternate personality, and he used it in various ways for self-promotion. His alternate personality claimed to be the reincarnation of an ancient executioner. Murphree suspected that in the boy's various readings of occult and demonic writings, he had come upon this "personality" as a fantasy he played out when it suited him. After all, he had convinced two teenage girls to have sex with him at the same time using the two alter-egos. What sixteen-year-old boy wouldn't like that?

Paul willingly told the Ranger what happened to the gun he had stolen from his father. It was in the attic of the house in The Parks of Roanoke, he said. He had opened the trapdoor on the second floor and had hidden the pistol up there in the attic. Murphree called the Roanoke police chief from his cell phone and told him what he had learned. Two officers drove to the still-empty house and climbed the stairs. They found the trapdoor to the attic and climbed up. As promised, the Ruger .22-caliber pistol, minus the magazine that Susan had found in Paul's packed luggage that Tuesday before her death, was there.

Murphree went back to the murder plot in his questioning. It was Jennifer's plan, Paul said. She wanted to kill her mother. She told him that, since his dad did not want them to be together either, they had to kill him too. And she told Merrilee White that Merrilee would never get away from her mother unless Amy too was dead. They needed to kill them all. They wanted to do it all on the Tuesday of that late September week. But when Merrilee tried to stab her mother that morning, got caught and was arrested, they were afraid she'd talk. The police would come for them soon, they thought. They sat around, fearfully waiting for the police to arrive at the door in the house at The Parks of Roanoke, but they never did. It looked like Merrilee had kept her mouth shut, they guessed. So they changed the date of their leaving to Thursday. David stayed home from school that day to be with them. He had been on in-school suspension anyway, and he never planned to return. He would be in Canada with his sister and her boyfriend. Like Merrilee, Paul didn't seem to have any real idea of what they would've done once they got to Canada. They would be friendless in another country, without work or study visas, and with no skills to offer an employer. Getting to Canada seemed to be the end of their planning.

Paul said that when Susan came in the front door that Thursday night, David hid in his room. Paul hid behind the half wall that separated the staircase from the game room. Jennifer waited to greet her mother in her bedroom door. When Susan reached the top of the stairs he came out from behind the wall and grabbed her.

"I just started stabbing and stabbing," Paul said. "Jennifer started stabbing her too."

And then David came out of his room with a knife and they all "blitzed" her until she was no longer moving. Paul had made the fatal stab wounds on the back of her head and neck and down her spinal cord. Jennifer had stabbed from the front and David had done only a few cuts on her chest. (Since those cuts did not appear to have bled, her heart had likely not been beating by then. But in the legal scheme of things, that didn't matter. David was as guilty as the others.)

Murphree listened to Paul's matter-of-fact recitation of the stabbing and was amazed at the words coming out of a teenager's mouth.

He asked about Paul's relationship with the two girls. They believed he had two personalities in the same body. They didn't look at the situation as one boy having two girlfriends. Jennifer was in love with Paul, and Merrilee was in love with Talos. Well, yes, he was having sex with both of them, sometimes at the same time, he admitted. He also encouraged them to have sex with each other while he watched.

"The hell you say," Murphree murmured.

Kate's Journal

———————

Thursday, October 15, 2009

I start writing. Am so emotional. Can't keep a sentence in line. My mind is jumping all around. What I want to say— how angry I am. Sad, hurt, disappointed, crying a lot. Feels like she, Jennifer, died.

30

Jennifer's Plea

A year had passed since her death, but Susan Bailey was never far from her mother's mind. Kate and Stephen Morten talked about the grandkids, about their daughter, trying to make sense of everything that had happened. They went round and round. Could Susan have done something to make her children hate her enough to kill her? They didn't think so. Jennifer was angry at her mother over Paul, but was that really enough to instill that kind of response? Jennifer didn't like having chores, but all kids had chores. And could David really have helped them? Kate remembered his sudden, angry response the day she hadn't bought him the snorkel he wanted. She'd been shocked by his reaction. But she never would have thought he could do something so cruel, so senseless, so violent. He was just a little kid.

Kate vacillated between loving and hating her grandchildren. They were her blood, her daughter's blood. She remembered when each of them was born, and she recalled the hard work her daughter had put herself through to support them with little help from their father. She remembered their sweet smiles, the hugs they gave her when they visited. She had looked forward to the adults they would become. Kate loved the children they had been. But the teens who had viscously stabbed her daughter more than two dozen times and left her lying on the floor while they took off for Canada? She wasn't sure she could ever love them again.

Detective Chris Almonrode had told Kate that prosecutors hoped she and Stephen would come down to Texas for Jennifer's trial, she wrote in her journal. Kate received a telephone call from an employee in the district attorney's office on October 6, 2009. Jennifer had agreed to enter a plea agreement to a reduced charge of murder and a sixty-year sentence, she learned. She was shocked, even though she had been expecting it. Sixty years! Kate would certainly be dead before her granddaughter saw freedom again. She received another call on October 14. The hearing was the next day, she was told. Could she and Stephen come?

Kate said no. It was too long a trip to plan and make in one day. Even driving hard, it was a two-day trip. It just wasn't possible.

Would she like to write an impact statement? The judge would read it to the defendant if Kate was not in the courtroom, the district attorney employee told her.

"I don't even know what that is!" she said.

The employee explained that Kate could tell Jennifer what she thought about her actions. She could tell her how much she had been hurt, how she couldn't forget how her daughter must have suffered at the hands of her own children. She could admonish Jennifer. The prosecutor would read it to the courtroom if she wrote the statement. Did she want to do that? Yes, she thought. She did.

Her husband didn't want to make a statement, Kate wrote in her journal. One of her sons said he just wanted the kids to die. She called Detective Peterson. He had taken a new job and was not going to be able to come to the hearing, he told her. But he encouraged her to write an impact statement.

"It is your last chance to tell Jennifer how you feel. Just pour your heart out to her."

Susan's friends Kim Aiken and Sheryl Barnes were going to make impact statements. Both of them talked to Kate on the telephone about their feelings for Susan and the way she had been killed. Kate broke down and cried. It was so hard.

But the hearing didn't take place the next day after all. The two friends called her and explained that the hearing had begun but the judge stopped it, they said. Jennifer was supposed to testify about her role in the murder. In order to get her crime reduced from capital murder to murder, she was supposed to admit that she had a part in the plan and that she had wielded a knife just as her brother and boyfriend had. She knew that when she climbed onto the witness stand. But she didn't do what she said she would. She testified that she and Merrilee made the plan in writing and gave it to David for safekeeping. If it had not happened in a week he was supposed to destroy the paper. She said David stayed in his room the whole time and had no involvement in the stabbing. She said her mother cried for her to call 911 but Paul prevented her from calling. He had unplugged the telephones in the house. Jennifer said she was a bystander and had watched in horror as Paul killed her mother while she begged him to stop.

She was lying, the prosecutor told the judge. Her testimony was not consistent with the evidence. This was a violation of her plea agreement. The judge told the bailiff to take Jennifer back to her cell. She hadn't kept her side of the bargain, and until or unless she did there would be no reduced sentence and she would go to trial. Jennifer would take her chances with a jury, who would look at the horrifying photographs of Susan dead in the hallway, of the knife and cell phones in the bloody bathtub, and then that jury would judge her. Sheryl told Kate that Jennifer broke down on the stand and started sobbing. They led her from the courtroom and Sheryl and Kim could hear her screaming in a back hallway. The judge had scheduled another hearing for Monday at eight A.M. If Jennifer did not tell the truth that day, the case would go to trial and the plea agreement would be nullified.

Prosecutor Victoria Abbott called Kate later that day. She asked if the Mortens could come to the hearing on Monday, October 19, 2009. She could not guarantee any different outcome than the one that had just occurred, she said. But she really wanted Susan's parents to be there. She wanted Jennifer to have to see them sitting there and listening to her talk about killing their daughter. If Jennifer lied again, she would face a capital murder trial in November, the prosecutor said.

Stephen didn't want to go. It would be a wasted trip, he said. But Kate wanted to hear what her granddaughter would have to say, and eventually he agreed to accompany her. One of her sons and his wife also wanted to attend, so they all left for Texas.

On October 19, 2009, Kate and Stephen Morten were in the courtroom to watch the plea hearing. Jennifer was sitting in the front of the courtroom with her back to the people seated there and didn't notice her grandparents at first. When she was called to the stand this time, Jennifer pled guilty to a reduced charge of murder—one step lower than capital murder—in return for a sixty-year sentence. Like Paul, she would need to serve at least half the sentence before becoming eligible for parole. And also like Paul, she had no assurance that she will be released the first time she becomes eligible, or at all until her sentence was completed in 2068. At that time she would be seventy-eight years old.

The Morten family listened to Jennifer's confession. This time she said that her mother came home just before midnight and they were going to watch movies together. David was asleep in his room, she said. It was doubtful that this was the truth, given Susan's long working day and the fact that she had to arise the next morning and go to work again. Jennifer said she went into the upstairs hall bathroom and found Paul up there. All the telephones in the house were unplugged, Jennifer testified. Paul was hiding in the game room and came out and began stabbing her mother, Jennifer said. She told him to stop but he said no and continued to use the knife. Paul started to "freak out," she told the judge. Her mother was dead.

"How did you know?" the prosecutor asked.

"I just knew," she said.

Her story laid a small amount of guilt on her own shoulders, for not stopping Paul or reporting the crime to the police. Again she insisted that David was in his room the whole time. Kate thought that there was little difference in the latest confession from the first one but the judge accepted it.

Kate wrote in her journal that Jennifer cried when her grandmother read her impact statement. Kate wasn't sure she really felt ashamed. She was probably grieving that she would have to spend most of her life in prison. Then Sheryl gave a statement and "really chewed her out." Jennifer cried harder, Kate wrote. Afterward, the prosecutors told the Mortens that Jennifer's testimony that her brother was not involved would probably help David get a shorter sentence. Kate wasn't sure how she felt about that.

Jennifer was quiet and kept to herself in the women's jail. A jailer's job is to watch over the inmates to make sure they are safe, to make sure they are not plotting to escape and to escort them from their cells to visitation, church programs or other self-help programs. They take meals on trays and slide them through "bean holes" in the cell doors. Then they make sure that each inmate returns the tray.

Jailers get to know the inmates they watch over very well and often bond with inmates. They don't want to know about their crimes because that might cause them to treat an inmate differently. But they need to know enough about their normal behavior to recognize when something is wrong or different.

For a while, Jennifer was in a block of eight cells with a catwalk around and through the block of cells. Each cell held one inmate, but the prisoners in each cell could talk among themselves. This was protective custody for high-profile inmates, and they were allowed one hour each day to leave the cell block and hang out in the dayroom. Two jailers who worked the three-to-eleven shift were intrigued by the girl and the crime she was accused of committing. She gave them no trouble. But neither were they fully convinced by her.

Jennifer was empty, the two guards said.

"Her eyes gave it away. She had no soul."

Jennifer never missed a church service, they noted. She participated in the religious services, but the jailers believed that was probably to help her case. This was common among inmates. Some found God and some only pretended.

"Maybe she was really looking, but I think she was one of those people who was not going to find what she was looking for," one of the jailers said.

Jennifer was moved to "general population" for a while. There she met another woman the jailers referred to as "butch." The two formed a relationship. Inmates in general population often form intimate relationships with each other because they have need of emotional and physical relationships and there are no men, the jailers said. Some of those women are sexual predators, always on the prowl for the frightened young women who are vulnerable to their attentions. No matter how butch or unattractive those women are, they always seem to be in a relationship, the guards said.

Women in general population look out for one another. If two women want a bit of privacy, others will watch and listen for guards. Some guards have a set routine. They make their rounds of the cells each half hour. The inmates soon learned which guards they could count on to stay away that long who they could take advantage of while others listened for footsteps down the catwalk. The inmates were canny, the jailers said. Inmates could tell which of the guards was coming by their perfume and the sounds they made walking by.

"They know your smell," one jailer said. "They know your walk. They know how you react."

Jennifer didn't stay in the general population area for long. She returned to the cell block with only one hour a day for recreation. The guards believed that it was at her own request. Once, a guard caught her trying to pass a note to the woman she had been in the relationship with. Written communication is not allowed, and the jailer gave her a verbal reprimand. Another incident like this and she would be issued a written reprimand, which would affect her status and privileges, the jailer told her. It did not happen again.

After Jennifer accepted the plea agreement, she changed. She had been living in some sort of dream world where this was not really happening and she would soon be able to go home, the jailers believed. Now, reality had sunk in. She was going to prison. Jennifer became depressed and unresponsive. Jail authorities took notice and gave her a box of colored pencils. Usually, an inmate must buy such an item from the commissary. But Jennifer had no one to place money in her commissary account. She was indigent. So she was given the colored pencils, and the ability to draw with them seemed to somewhat lift her from the depression.

Shortly after she pled out, Jennifer agreed to be interviewed by journalism students from her alma mater, Northwest High School. Journalism teacher Betty Johnson Roberts accompanied students Sarah Johnston and Lauren Hoffmann to the Denton County Jail. They were allowed into a room with a telephone on one side of a glass window. Jennifer sat on the other side with another telephone. It would be their form of communication. They could see her through the glass. They could hear her, one at a time, on the telephone. But she may as well have been on television. She was so far removed from them and their teenage daily lives that it was hard for the girls to fathom what it would be like to be locked inside a building all day, every day.

Sarah interviewed Jennifer while Lauren shot photographs through the window. It was their first visit to such a facility, and they were wide-eyed. Later, Sarah's story and Lauren's photograph appeared in the school newspaper, the *Texas Times*. First, however, the school's lawyer had to vet the story to make sure that nothing Jennifer said or that Sarah wrote would get the school in legal trouble.

Jennifer wore an orange jail jumpsuit and her long hair was pulled back from her face. She knew people thought of her as a murderer, she said. But that could not be avoided. No one could hurt her now, she explained. She said she signed the plea agreement to avoid life in prison without parole. At least that way there was a possibility that she would one day be released. She attributed the sentence to God's mercy.

Jennifer had found God in county jail, she said, and she referred to her faith throughout the interview. She said she went to church in the jail every Sunday and to Bible study every Monday. She was a born-again Christian, and she relied on God to help her through her incarceration. Soon she would be transferred to the Mountain View Unit in Gatesville, Texas, where many of the state's female prisoners are confined.

Jennifer didn't want to talk about the actual killing of her mother. But she did speak of the Sunday morning that their car was stopped in Yankton, South Dakota. It was "a God-given gift that we were pulled over at four in the morning," she told the high school reporter, not explaining what she meant by that.

Jennifer spun a tale for the reporter about growing up in a mentally abusive household. No one knew about this abuse because it was done behind closed doors, she said.

"My brother and I were slaves to the house," she said.

She said the house always had to be clean to Susan's satisfaction before she and her brother could leave it. The high school girls had not had the advantage of seeing photos of the incredibly messy house police found after the teens killed Susan, but if they had they would have known that if Susan actually enforced such rules, they certainly were not followed whenever the police or her relatives had visited, nor the last time her children left the house.

Jennifer claimed that she had not been able to attend her senior prom because her mother had spent money on something else instead. The massive telephone bill Jennifer and her brother had racked up, perhaps? Then where had the rose-colored beaded gown and the prom picture of her and Paul come from? The reporter did not know about the prom picture.

Jennifer said her mother repeatedly called David "stupid."

She told the girls that her father was denied the right to see his children because of past violent abuse. The high school girls had no way to know that this was not true. The truth was that Susan had asked for full custody in her divorce petition. Since Richard Bailey had not hired a lawyer or made any effort to contest the divorce, Susan was granted full custody.

Jennifer placed the blame for Susan's murder on Paul. But she blamed herself for not stopping him, she said. And she never wanted to see him again. If she could, she would tell Susan how sorry she was, she told the young reporter. She should have listened when her mother told her that Paul was bad news, Jennifer said. It was because of Paul that she was locked in a jailhouse.

Yes, she had been almost eighteen years old when the murder happened. She could have just walked away at that time. But she couldn't leave her little brother there to face the emotional abuse, she said. So she took him with her on the aborted trip to Canada.

Jennifer told Sarah that she hoped to take some

psychology courses when she arrived at the Gatesville, Texas, prison unit. She wanted to help other people who had been through the abuse she had suffered, she said.

She also told the young reporter that she was taking anti-depressants. She spent time in her cell alone and she thought back to that day.

"[I have to live] with the fact that I watched my mom die," Jennifer said.

31

Reactions from Officers

The Bailey case received some television news coverage and the plea bargains were recounted in newspaper reports. Then it faded from the headlines. But in January 2012, the Investigation Discovery channel aired a segment of *Deadly Women* that featured the Susan Bailey murder case. Neighbor Michelle Davidson and Denton County First Assistant District Attorney Jaime Beck appear, and the rest is reenacted using actors. The neighbor says she had watched Jennifer walk home from school by herself, reading a book. She was a quiet girl, the neighbor says. But she had a boyfriend whom her mother didn't like.

Beck calls Paul Henson Jr. a goth and says the two sweethearts were "dabbling with the devil."

The reenactment shows a Jennifer with braces and an actor portraying Paul wearing a black cape and leaping about while Jennifer looked on in admiration. The moderator calls him a "warlock." The reenactment shows Jennifer stabbing her mother repeatedly and Paul holding a baseball bat. In the reenactment, the teens are stopped in Yankton by a police officer, and they tell him they are "heading home."

The show uses phrases like "going to the dark side," "a natural-born killer" and "the murder plot unravels."

The only mention of David is that he was an "innocent child" who got dragged into a murder.

Another television show on the Investigation Discovery channel called *Facing Evil* covered the Susan Bailey case. This show features television personality Candice DeLong interviewing Jennifer in jail.

"She saw her mother stabbed with her own eyes," DeLong says of Jennifer.

That program also uses actors to demonstrate the murder. Jennifer tells DeLong that she walked up the stairs with her mother, and as she did, she realized that the plot to kill her was wrong. She decided to tell her mother that Paul planned to kill her, Jennifer says, with tears in her eyes. But when she went into one of the upstairs bathrooms, she heard her mother screaming. Jennifer claims that she walked out and saw that Paul had her mother against the wall, holding a knife to her throat. Susan screamed to her daughter to call police.

"I said no," Jennifer admits, crying prettily.

"You said no," DeLong states.

"I said no," Jennifer repeats.

She doesn't know why she did that, Jennifer says. But Paul looked at her and told her not to call, so she didn't. Then she watched Paul slice her mother's throat.

"He grinned while he did it," Jennifer recalls with big, sad eyes.

"He grinned?"

"He grinned."

In the reenactment, Paul looks menacingly at Susan as he holds a knife to her throat while Jennifer cowers down the hall.

When Kate and Stephen Morten watched these programs about the murder of their daughter, they were appalled. The couple had never really thought in detail about the crime. Not about each stab wound. Not about which teen had done which awful thing. Seeing reenactments brought the horror of the whole thing right into Kate's heart. Her grandchildren had done this! Her grandchildren had hurt Susan. They had terrorized her. They had murdered her!

Yankton, South Dakota, Officer Eric Kolda was equally disturbed as he watched Jennifer's interview on *Facing Evil* at his home. He now knew the whole story, and this was not it. Not even close.

"I wanted to go through that TV and grab her," he said later. "I sent an e-mail to that show and told them they let her off easy. She was not innocent. They should have talked to someone who was there. They called David an innocent child. That 'child' was just as much a part of it as the rest of them. I believe they would have killed their grandma and grandpa if they had not been stopped. I beg the state of Texas to never let them out. It would be a disgrace to their mother if they walked among us."

Kolda was not the only officer who reacted to the pleas and the television shows. Larry Kish later moved from crime-scene investigation to a job as a regular detective at the Denton County Sheriff's Office and in 2012 was promoted to detective sergeant. His expertise in crime-scene investigation stood him in good stead on all his cases and in his role of supervising detectives and crime-scene technicians. He had worked a lot of cases; he had seen a lot of bodies. But the Susan Bailey case never really left his mind. He had three children of his own, and he could not fathom any of them participating in such violence as he had seen at the house in The Parks at Roanoke.

Kish has blond hair and blue eyes and his skin is very fair. A blush is quite evident, and when he talks about the detective's role in the case of a homicide, a red flush creeps up his neck and into his face. Kish cares. He talked about the three youngsters involved in the death of Susan Bailey. He believed that Jennifer was the brains behind the attack. She was the one who wanted her mother dead. She most likely inflicted the wounds on one side of Susan's chest. They were not as deep and contained hesitation marks. The five light wounds on the other side of Susan's chest he attributed to David. Both Jennifer and David were too small to inflict the worst damage to the body of someone as large as Susan, he said. He pictured Paul, a strapping sixteen-year-old, as the brawn behind the cut throat, the deep stab wounds in her back. Three different knives and three different styles of handling the knives had been apparent, he thought.

The detectives had all worked long hours with little sleep until they'd felt they had the case under control. But they were not willing to slow down until they were sure the teens were under arrest. They owed that to Susan Bailey, Kish explained.

"Investigators are the last force acting for the victims," he said. "You have to be very seriously dedicated. You have to work as long as it takes. That's our job. We are the voice for that victim."

Kish said some victims are the lowest of the low, drug dealers who kill one another over their ill-gotten gains. Some victims are honest, hardworking people and a few victims are rich, high-profile people.

"When they're dead, it doesn't matter," he said. "We work hard. We get results."

Crime-scene investigators go through hundreds of extra training hours to learn such specific investigative tools as blood-spatter analysis and collection of latent fingerprints. They learn the proper way to collect evidence so as not to contaminate it and to preserve it so that defense lawyers can't have it thrown out. But the most important quality in an investigator is common sense, Kish said. Some cops call it "old school" investigating.

"It's plain old common sense. You can't learn it. And you can't replace it with anything else."

Roanoke Police Chief Gary Johnson made their job so much easier, he said. He set up their "war room" with everything they could possibly need and he opened his budget to make that happen.

"He said, 'The bottom line is, we gotta solve this murder.'"

And solve it they did. Kish took numerous items to the lab for DNA testing, and that was an expensive budget item.

Johnson had tightened his lips when he heard just how expensive a budget item it would be, but he'd okayed the expenditure. The more they found out, the more sure they were that they could get convictions in the murder case. If Paul tried to say he hadn't participated, they had his fingerprints in the blood and his DNA on the frayed wire of the extension cord. If Jennifer protested that Paul was the only killer, they could prove her wrong. These kids thought they had planned the crime well and that they could get away and never be found. They were wrong. Even without Officer Kolda's good police work, they would eventually have found those kids and nailed them, Kish said.

Kish still shakes his head when he thinks about Paul and Jennifer and David.

"I still can't wrap my head around kids who kill."

32

The Letters

Kate Morten and her granddaughter exchanged a few letters early on, but then correspondence between them dried up until November 4, 2010.

Jennifer Bailey wrote a brief note to her grandmother from the Mountain View Unit of the Texas prison system in Gatesville. She wrote that she knew her grandmother was hurting and wanted nothing to do with her. "I'm sorry things happened the way they did," she wrote, the best attempt at saying she was sorry that she had made to that day. "But I'm grateful for it because it led me to Jesus." She told her grandmother that Jesus loved her and she made a drawing of a cross with flowers adorning the top and a heart in the middle with "Jesus" on it. She was practicing her artistic talent with what little she had to do it with.

Kate was skeptical about the religious transformation,

but she was willing to give her granddaughter the benefit of the doubt.

In May 2011, Kate received a fat envelope from Jennifer. First she pulled out of the envelope an elaborate, detailed pen-and-ink drawing that was merely decorative in nature. In the middle, she had penned "Happy Mother's Day." This drawing was for the mother she had killed years earlier.

Next Kate found two letters printed on the back and front of the same sheet of paper. Each was addressed to "Mama."

The first one, dated May 25, 2011, began, "Not a day goes by that I don't think of you at least once." She respected her now, Jennifer wrote. She missed her terribly. She begged her mother for forgiveness, though still implying that her sin was of omission. She should have told Susan what Paul was planning, she wrote.

The next day, Jennifer wrote another letter on the back of the first one. Again she asked for forgiveness. "Mom, you know what happened that night," she wrote. "To this day it haunts me. What happened was so horrendous and brutal. But above all it was cruel and extremely wrong."

Jennifer wrote that she hoped her mother was proud of her for accepting the consequences of her actions. She had taken a great leap forward, she wrote. She was no longer bitter toward Susan or her dad. She wrote that Susan once asked her why she was so angry with her parents and that her mother had listened when she told her and that Susan had changed some of the things that made her daughter angry. Her mother had always been there for her, Jennifer wrote.

"I still feel your love for me and David. Please forgive us."

Finally, the envelope contained a letter to Kate from

Jennifer. It repeated some of the things she had written to her mother. At least, she wrote, her mom was now with Jesus, with no more worries about bills or what her children were doing.

"She is now resting in Heaven, having the time of her life with Jesus."

Jennifer asked her grandmother for photographs of the family and of her mother. She asked her to keep the Mother's Day card and letters that she'd written to Susan. She believed they would mean a lot to Kate.

But a month later, Jennifer's mood seemed to have changed. In a letter dated June 10, 2011, she began by saying that she realized that "sorry" would never be enough for her grandmother and that she doubted that she even existed for Kate anymore.

But then Jennifer launched into a diatribe of all the perceived slights she and her family had suffered from her grandparents. She believed the Mortens had never forgiven their daughter for moving to California and marrying Richard. Kate hadn't treated them well because of that, she wrote.

"Grandma, I'm going to be honest. I've never forgiven you because of how you treated my mom, dad and brother for the longest time."

She wrote that Kate had treated her family "like dirt" and "you just brushed my dad off like he was a big, stupid lug."

She recalled her twelfth birthday, when they were visiting the Mortens in Minnesota. Kate had made her daughter and son-in-law stay in one of the lodge cabins the couple owned instead of in her house, she wrote, though she allowed Jennifer and David to stay in the house with her. She believed that was because her parents had not moved up north to live near the rest of the family. Jennifer also resented the fact that it was only after her parents divorced that Kate was much more interested in seeing them and helping her mother.

"You are going to have to realize you are not the only one suffering," she wrote to Kate.

Her father had still loved her mother and grieved over Susan as well, Jennifer claimed. She said that she still had nightmares about that night her mother died, and she worried that David was suffering too. She believed that she was all David had, yet they could not be together. She wrote about her mother's "cruelty" in making David wear diapers at night because he wet the bed. Her grandmother just never saw things from her and David's point of view. Even though she had been angry with her grandmother for such a long time, Jennifer wrote, she still loved her. She ended the letter with "God bless you."

She included drawings of a puppy and a teddy bear with her letter.

Kate waited ten days to reply. She needed the time to let her anger subside somewhat before she wrote back. "At least you wrote a letter that I can respond to," she began. "It was full of emotion and fantasy stories to fit your mood."

Kate wrote that she knew Jennifer had spent too much time in the house taking care of David because Susan had to work so many hours. She had tried to tell Susan and Richard that, she wrote, but they hadn't listened. She knew that Jennifer began to live her life through fantasy books and movies. She and Stephen had visited as much as they could afford to, and she'd personally taken over Jennifer's chores while she was there. She'd also tried to teach Jennifer some things that would have made her life easier. But Jennifer had not been interested in learning and had only wanted to complain.

Kate acknowledged that Susan and Richard were not close to the rest of the Morten family when they lived in California. She told her granddaughter that it had been her father's choice for Susan and him to stay in the cabin that year Jennifer was twelve. They could have stayed in the family house, but he hadn't wanted to, she wrote. Kate wrote that she believed Jennifer did not understand why David had been allowed to stay with his grandparents that last summer. Jennifer was supposed to be working, and Susan did not want him to be at home alone. Kate said they'd agreed to keep him for a month to see how things went. But by the time a month had passed, David had a very serious, potentially deadly staph infection with seven or eight lesions, she said. They were trying hard to heal the lesions, but he picked at them and kept them open. She didn't think they could allow him to go home and stay alone so much with such a serious infection. She believed that neither Jennifer nor Susan realized the seriousness of the MRSA infection. She was sorry that Jennifer took their wanting to keep David longer the wrong way. She thought Jennifer had been jealous.

Susan had hoped she could get closer to her daughter while just the two of them were living in the house. Jennifer had been forbidden to see Paul. But Susan told her mother via telephone conversations that all Jennifer was doing was moping around the house carrying a teddy bear that Paul had given her. Susan didn't know what to do, so she allowed her daughter to see Paul. "BIG MISTAKE," Kate wrote.

"I am haunted with the reasons for your actions against

your mother & believe they were because of Paul. I don't really hate you. I am still numb. I am having a hard time understanding why and what led to the planning. You were caught in too many lies is my guess."

The two exchanged angry letters again in July 2011. Jennifer wrote nearly five pages on cheap prison paper with a pencil so dull it was impossible to decipher in many places. She took exception to her grandmother's last letter and accused her of being on her "high-and-mighty horse."

She wrote that her mother never made the "big mistake" her grandmother had written about. Susan never liked Paul and never accepted him or let him in, she said. It was she, Jennifer, who made the big mistake, she wrote. She should have warned her mother that Paul, and even David, were talking about killing her. Jennifer vacillated between blaming her mother and grandmother for perceived wrongs, and asking for forgiveness. She wrote that she had been baptized and that God was in her life now.

"What brought it all to a head was the fact that Paul's dad had forbidden him to ever see me again."

She wrote her grandmother that she hoped their relationship could heal in time and she looked forward to hearing from Kate again. She signed it "Love, Jennifer." Underneath she drew a lovely flower with her dull pencil.

Her grandmother replied, again pointing out the inconsistencies in the letter she had received. Jennifer both complained that her grandparents came to visit and then that they didn't come enough. They visited once a year because that was as often as they could afford the long trip, she explained. She always gave Susan notice far in advance so that she could perhaps take time off from work. But her daughter always worked the whole length of the visit, and she and Stephen had nothing to do.

She took offense at her granddaughter's declaration in one of her letters that Jennifer hated her.

"You didn't know me enough to hate," she wrote.

A different Jennifer wrote to her grandmother in October 2011. She said she was sorry to learn that her last letter came off as mean. She didn't plan it that way. This letter was chatty. She said she missed her mother every day. She said she had been working in the kitchen for two years and that she liked the work and her bosses, but she didn't like most of the other inmates. They complained constantly.

She asked about various family members and asked for another photograph of David. She wanted to draw a picture from the photo and send it to Kate, she wrote. She wished she could take college classes in a program for inmates. But because of the seriousness of her crime, she was not allowed to leave the unit and was not allowed to apply for a grant to pay for the college classes.

Jennifer wrote that she was attending a program that was helping her to move forward. She was learning that she wasn't the only person to make a really bad mistake. She deserved the death penalty for what she did, Jennifer wrote. She considered the sixty-year sentence a second chance.

She addressed the murder in vague terms. "It" was all Paul's idea, she wrote. She and David only went along with it because they were under his control. Now neither of them wanted much to do with him.

Included in this envelope was a lovely birthday card

Jennifer made for her grandmother on stiffer paper than the flimsy stuff of her letters. It was done in colored pencils and showed pretty butterflies and flowers. Jennifer really did have artistic talent. It read in part, "Blessings on your birthday!"

The envelope also contained a poem and an essay that had been written by inmates and printed in the prison newspaper. And last was a photo that someone had taken of Jennifer and Richard inside a fenced area at the Mountain View Unit in Gatesville.

The last letter to Kate arrived in early January 2012. It contained an assortment of pages. There were five pages of instructions for crocheting and several drawings illustrating the patterns. She thought her grandmother would like to crochet something using the patterns. There was a drawing of a puppy chewing on a bone. There were five tiny pages about four by six inches that had been torn from a larger sheet of paper. This was Jennifer's letter to Kate.

The letter began with thanks to her grandmother for the Christmas card and the crocheted cross she'd sent her. The cross was beautiful, but the prison authorities would not allow her to keep it. She wrote that she'd sent the cross to her father so that he could take a photograph of it and mail that back to her. The photo, at least, she would be allowed to keep in her cell. She wrote that her father would take good care of the cross for her.

Her father had visited on Christmas Eve, Jennifer wrote. Richard softened when she told him that her grandmother had sent her family photos and a birthday card. She wished the two of them could get along, she wrote. They were all she had.

Jennifer reminisced about a Christmas they all had spent together. It had been wonderful, she wrote, and she'd dreamed about it. She wrote about a "Bridge to Life" class she'd recently graduated from. She'd learned a lot.

She wrote that the class had "helped me understand yours and everyone else's side of not only feelings but how horrible it all looks, sounds and seems to be because it really is."

She was worried that David had been placed in a program that forced him to talk about what happened that night in the upstairs hallway. He was asking her questions about it because he actually didn't remember it. She wasn't sure what effect the program was going to have on him.

The drama was high in her unit, she wrote. It was like high school but worse, because they all had to live close together. Some of the women acted masculine. They were called "stud broads," Jennifer wrote.

She wished her grandmother a happy New Year.

Kate could not decide what to do about her granddaughter. On one hand, she loved her. She was Susan's daughter. On the other hand, Jennifer had cold-bloodedly stabbed her own mother to death. How could she forgive that? Kate wrestled with the issue. Jennifer could sometimes sound contrite about her crime. Other times she blamed Paul, as though she had taken no part in it. Sometimes Jennifer's letters were loving and full of hope that they could someday have a real relationship again. But on bad days, Jennifer was angry and bitter and mean.

The letters upset Kate. She sent some photographs of the extended family from their last Christmas together. She wasn't about to send any of Susan. Jennifer didn't deserve those. She looked through the small amount of Susan's jewelry she had kept, looking for the pearl earrings and necklace Jennifer had described as having belonged to Richard's mother. She saw nothing like that in the things she had saved. Either they had been given to the charity for resale with the rest of Susan's costume jewelry or something else had happened to them. She was not in touch with Richard and didn't intend to be, so she didn't worry about it.

The letters Jennifer sent to her that she had written to Susan set Kate back on her heels. What on earth? She had no idea why the girl would have written the letters or why she sent them to her grandmother. Maybe she just wanted to have them for safekeeping, Kate decided. In the event that she was released on parole she could retrieve them. Kate didn't much like all the religious talk. These letters were not about Jennifer and her grandmother. They had a phony ring to them. They made her uncomfortable. And she never knew whether she was going to pull a syrupy, apologetic tome in an envelope or a spiteful, accusing letter that seemed to place the blame for her plight on her grandmother.

Kate also tried to write to David. He sent a couple of short notes back, but he was mostly begging her not to tell his father that he had written to her.

Kate stopped writing in 2012. It was just too hard.

A Letter from Kate

Tuesday, August 19, 2014

I have not corresponded with Jennifer for two years and David only twice. I read the letters again for the first time since receiving them. Guess I'm still not ready to forgive her. So sad.

33

The Units

The state of Texas has a huge corrections system. Texas is the second-largest state in the United States, with only Alaska surpassing it in square miles if not in population, and it houses numerous prisoners. The Texas Department of Criminal Justice has a hundred and ten prisons in which inmates are incarcerated, and they are located all over the state. A few of these are privately run and contracted to the state for their services. Most are run by state employees. The vast majority house male inmates. Seven house females and two are co-gender units.

Jennifer Bailey was sent to Gatesville to the Mountain View Unit. Gatesville is a small town in Central Texas where six prisons provide work for many of the people who live there. One state jail and four men's prisons are there in addition to the largest women's prison in the state. It has a capacity for six hundred and forty-five inmates and employs three hundred people. Women sentenced to die reside in their own death row inside Mountain View.

Texas executes its death row inmates by lethal injection, and that was what Jennifer feared most and avoided partly because she turned eighteen only ten days after her mother was so brutally murdered. Had she reached her eighteenth birthday before she helped stab her mother to death, she might have realized that nightmare. Texas has one of the highest incidences of lethal punishment in death penalty cases in the country. In November 2014 there were two hundred and seventy-three inmates on Texas's death row, including seven women.

Instead of "riding the needle," as lethal injection is sometimes called, Jennifer was sent to a unit where women could raise crops and swine on the ninety-seven acres of the prison. There also is a farm shop and a Braille facility, where inmates make books for the blind. Jennifer had written her grandmother that she worked as a cook at first and that she liked the work. She was taking some faith-based courses but was not allowed to attend colleges or apply for grants to pay for them because of the severity of her crime. Some colleges in Texas's state-college system offered courses to inmates who were bussed away from their units to attend, but murderers were kept inside the fences and the concertina wire. So Jennifer's hope of taking psychology courses would not be realized.

Paul Henson Jr. had been taken to the Mark W. Stiles Unit in Jefferson County near Beaumont. It is a male-only prison with a maximum population of almost three thousand. It comprises seven hundred and seventy-six acres, most of it used for gardens. Inmates raise vegetables that are then hauled away and cooked in other prisons. The inmates also provide laundry service for a nearby state jail as well as for other inmates at Stiles. State jails house offenders who have committed lesser crimes than the felons who are incarcerated in the prisons and are intended to relieve crowding in the felony prisons. The state jails offer a less restrictive incarceration.

Paul's projected release date was September 28, 2068, but he could be released on parole as early as September 28, 2038.

David Bailey was the last to enter a plea. On October 28, 2009, he entered into a plea agreement in juvenile court. He pled guilty to the reduced charge of murder in return for a twenty-six-year determinant sentence. He would remain in a juvenile facility until he turned eighteen years of age. Then there would be a hearing, and a judge would decide whether he should be released at that time or whether he would be transported to an adult prison unit in the Texas Department of Criminal Justice.

That hearing took place soon after he turned eighteen. He came of age in 2013 and, after a hearing in Denton County, the judge ruled that he would continue to be incarcerated until either his sentence was completed or he was released on parole.

David was taken to the Clemens Unit in Brazoria County, which is near Angleton, below Houston on the Texas Gulf Coast. It primarily houses youthful offenders, but others who are under administrative segregation and many "trusties" live there as well. The unit encompasses eight thousand acres.

Inmates there raise horses, cattle and swine. They also work in the fields where grain is raised, and there is a storage facility on the grounds for storing grain. David would have an opportunity there to obtain a GED.

His projected release date is October 7, 2034 but he becomes eligible for parole in 2021. The law enforcement officers don't think he will be paroled that soon.

He was moved to the Clemens Unit to finish his sentence. The unit houses a maximum eight hundred and ninety-four inmates who are either youthful offenders or segregated for some other reason from the general population. There also is a "trusty" camp there where inmates in the trusty program are given more freedom. Trusties are inmates who have earned favor by their hard work, the self-improvement programs they attend and their adherence to the rules. Violent offenders are not eligible for trusty status. Inmates raise beef cattle, crops and swine and there are programs to teach bricklaying and construction. Brazoria County is near Houston, about two hundred and forty-five miles from Gatesville. But David and his sister may as well have been in different countries. Texas comprises nearly two hundred and seventy thousand square miles.

Mountain View in Gatesville, where Jennifer is incarcerated, and the Clemens Unit appear fairly close on a Texas map, but Texas is a huge state. The units are actually a four-hour drive—two hundred and forty-five miles—apart and the siblings cannot visit each other.

But David wrote to his grandmother that his dad visited both of them at first and carried messages between them. And they were allowed to write letters to each other, so they did have some connection. Richard Bailey's sister, Cindy Bruns, sent money now and then to their commissary accounts to buy small items not provided by the state. She placed money in their prison accounts, so they were occasionally able to call her. Richard's sister says that he suffered post-traumatic stress disorder after his children murdered his former wife, and he does not work, so he is not able to contribute to Jennifer's and David's prison accounts. They are considered indigent and cannot purchase from the prison commissary many items most people would deem essential to normal lives. Inmates with money in their prison accounts can purchase fruit juice, some snacks, tennis shoes, thermal clothing in winter, writing materials and stamps, and locks to keep their few belongings safe from theft.

Jennifer and David subsist mostly on the rations issued to indigent inmates.

34

Why?

Why did Jennifer and David Bailey kill their mother? Why did Paul Henson Jr. kill Susan and plan to kill his father? Why did Merrilee White attempt to stab her mother?

There is no definitive answer.

Tracy Murphree, Larry Kish, Brian Peterson and the Roanoke officers who worked the case think that it was Jennifer who wanted her mother dead. They believe that she influenced her young brother and manipulated her boyfriend with sex and by playing into his weird beliefs of reincarnation and demon worship.

Merrilee tried to assault her mother out of desperation because she so badly wanted to go along on the trip to Canada, the officers suspect, and David was young and looked at Jennifer as a mother figure. He wanted to please her. He was too young to understand the finality of death and simply went along with his beloved older sister, some believe—not that that makes him any less guilty in the eyes of the law.

Jennifer's high school friend Harley believed that Jennifer was a normal, happy girl who was influenced by the dark, troubled sixteen-year-old boy she thought she loved. Their friends at school were not all that surprised to learn that Paul had committed murder. But they were shocked and could not believe that Jennifer had participated. They thought she'd seemed just like every other teenage girl.

Jennifer was seventeen—almost eighteen—at the time of the murder, but was she really mature enough to understand that, unlike in the movies, a person stabbed twenty-six times will remain dead forever?

Jennifer changed her story a few times since the murder of her mother. She said Paul called her one day and told her that Susan's death needed to happen so they could be together. But, she said that the whole time they planned the stabbing, she only ever thought it was just talk and didn't really believe that Paul would go through with it. But she admitted that when her mother begged her to call police, she said no. Then she said that she tried to call but couldn't, because Paul had unplugged the telephones in the house. Is any part of that the truth? Was David a willing coconspirator or an innocent bystander?

Susan's mother, Kate Morten, still cannot fathom what happened to her once-loving grandchildren.

The truth is, no one knows what caused four youngsters to enter a conspiracy to murder their parents. And even experts disagree about what can go wrong in a child's life to produce such an aberration.

In Michael D. Kelleher's book, *When Good Kids Kill*, he writes that in many instances the real reason never emerges. He writes that there are several factors, however, that form a pattern in the stories of young killers like these. He lists:

A history of abuse in childhood

A father figure who may be absent, non-nurturing or passive

A mother who may be dominant, overprotective or seductive

There is violence in the home

Children experience a deep sense of abandonment and distrust

Mothers may experience fear of their children

There is no proven abuse in the Bailey family history. In the one instance when something David wrote aroused the suspicions of school officials, a police investigation determined that there was no evidence, in fact, of inappropriate touching or behavior. But Richard Bailey was absent for long stretches of his children's lives after the divorce, which occurred two years before the murder. Before he left, he did not allow his children outdoors if neither parent was present, Susan said. But was that overprotectiveness? Did the Bailey youngsters get conflicting emotional cues from their parents as to their being loved and protected?

Jennifer resented the fact that she so often had to babysit her younger brother, even when she knew that the reason her mother was away so much was due to her working at least one extra job. She did seem to feel abandoned and given too much responsibility. She claimed to be "a slave to the house," even though it did not appear that she did much to care for it. A classmate told police that "Jennifer loved to hate her mother."

Many, many children have one or more of these factors in their lives and yet never show violence, experts agree. And a large number of kids who do kill have none of these factors in their backgrounds. "When an adolescent rages out of control, he can become a ruthless, lethal murderer of the most brutal type," writes Kelleher. "His actions are often inexplicable, unreasonable and beyond the comprehension of most adults. This is frequently the reality with which we . . . must grapple."

It is commonly accepted that many teens go through periods of moodiness, complaining, slamming doors and yelling. But, according to Kelleher, there is extreme behavior that may come before a violent episode, including (but not limited to): abandoning old friends; a drop in grades; rapid mood swings; increasing defiance of rules; increasing conflict with authority figures; increasing secretiveness; or profound laziness or disinterest in normal activities.

The American Psychological Association also lists eight warning signs of imminent violence in teens. They are: frequent loss of temper; fighting; use of drugs; risk-taking behavior; detailed planning to commit violence; threats; hurting animals and carrying weapons.

It is certainly not a given that such behavior is leading to violence. But authorities agree that it can be a sign that something stressful is occurring in the lives of youngsters who exhibit these actions, and they may need to talk to a trusted adult or even a professional.

Looking back on the Bailey story, some of these warning signs were present. According to their friends, Paul became increasingly violent at school in the weeks before the stabbing. David seemed to always be fighting with bigger boys. Paul stole his father's pistol and David brought a knife to school. And when Jennifer was on the witness stand at her plea hearing, she said that she and Merrilee had written up a plan to kill their parents and had given it to David to hold for them. Merrilee told the Fort Worth officers that there had been a plan and that if Paul had a gun, the plan was in motion.

Parricide is not a major category of crime among juveniles. Fewer than ten percent of kids who kill murder their parents. Most young killers kill friends or schoolmates (as demonstrated in frightening cases in recent years of kids coming to school with weapons and opening fire). Statistics also show that these killers are mostly boys. They usually are Caucasian, middle class and of above-average intelligence. Usually, they have no criminal record and not much history of prior violence. But they often are from single-parent families.

The teen years are hard for most, and research shows that youngsters who kill their parents often don't have the attention of their parents and sometimes shoulder too much responsibility in the home. Like Jennifer, they may resent the absent parents and grow more and more angry because they must act as a caregiver or housekeeper.

"In fact, the typical perpetrator of parricide does not come close to satisfying the average American's assumption about most killers," Kelleher writes. "This is especially true when the issue of motivation is considered. Certainly, these raging, violent adolescents are rarely psychopathic murderers, although they occasionally murder for money, freedom or possessions."

Kelleher warns that these killers are not career criminals in the strictest form of the idea. They often are described by those who knew them as nonviolent and stable, he writes. Peers and people close to them often describe young killers as having been upstanding individuals.

"And in fact, perpetrators of parricide are often just that."

When detectives look back into the histories of children who kill their parents, they often find that the children complained about their parents to their friends beforehand, Kelleher writes. Several of Jennifer's friends told police that she was angry about having to take care of housework—one of them saying "she loved to hate her mother"—but none of them suspected that she might actually commit violence against her. But many more teens complain about their parents than actually kill them, the expert wrote.

"The fact that an adolescent complains bitterly about his parents, or even threatens in the presence of friends to kill them, does not necessarily indicate that he or she will do so," Kelleher says. Sometimes it is only braggadocio.

A second area of concern in children who kill is psychological disorder. According to the Kelleher book, police, the legal system and psychologists often disagree as to whether short-term psychological disorders are at the root of many parricides. Statistics show that more than half of them take place during an argument. It is not so much planned, in those cases, as an angry response. When kids kill, nearly two-thirds use a firearm. Paul had a pistol at one time, though police found the gun in one place and the magazine and ammunition in another, rendering it useless.

None of this sheds much light on the question of motivation. And the perpetrators themselves often provide little help with discovering exactly why the crimes were committed. Many of them were considered nonviolent, happy, stable kids. Jennifer and David displayed few of the hot-button signs of future violence. Paul was considered by his peers to be weird and outlandish. Most were not surprised when he acted violently. Did he lead the other two into murder? Some schoolmates believe that Jennifer was a happy, normal girl who was fascinated with things that she had never dealt with before and agreed to act out one of Paul's fantasies. But officers who investigated the case believe that Jennifer found a disturbed young man who had fantasies of blood and death and manipulated him into helping her commit the horrendous crime. David and Merrilee appear to all who have studied the case to have been children who became caught up in something they were not mature enough to understand, but who went along with it because of their loyalty to the older youths and their own curiosity about the dark fantasies they'd heard about.

After they were captured, Jennifer and Paul showed little to no remorse. Was it a tough front, or were they actually without conscience? Freudian concepts present the human conscience as the superego. Are children who kill born without a conscience? Does the superego fail to imprint the lessons learned in childhood? Psychologists ask, if these children do have a conscience, what kept it from preventing them from committing the worst of all crimes? Something stronger then conscience—hatred and rage, at least for the time it took to commit the crime—intervened.

Jennifer vacillated in her letters to her grandmother between saying she was sorry and blaming her boyfriend or even her mother.

According to Kelleher, there is little evidence that most of the youngsters who kill are born with a personality disorder. There is no evidence that any of the three who stabbed Susan Bailey lacked a sound upbringing. All three of Susan's killers appeared to have been taught right from wrong, and they had mostly listened to their consciences all their lives until that moment.

Even among experts, "Born or bred?" is a question that still has not been answered. Does society or family create sociopaths? Are they born with something missing? Is it genetic? How great a role does environment play? What in the environment of the Bailey house or the Henson house could have taught them to kill?

Kelleher writes that a genuine sociopath usually has a long history of increasingly aberrant behavior. Neither Jennifer nor David nor Paul fits this picture.

Will society ever know without qualifications what causes seemingly good kids to kill? Will anyone ever know for sure why these teens killed Susan Bailey? The answer is: it is doubtful, at best.

However, there are things the detectives found out that might partially explain these children's behavior. Jennifer resented her mother, as teenage girls often do for a few years. She believed she should not have had to keep the house clean. She was not allowed much freedom because she was responsible for her younger brother. The resentment festered in Jennifer.

Paul brought strange new ideas into Jennifer's life. It is doubtful that she ever gave much thought to reincarnation or to the practice of witchcraft or to demons before she entered a relationship with him. She admits to a fascination with those aspects of his personality. Jennifer found love, but she also found the solution to her problem. She wanted freedom. She wanted her mother dead. Paul was willing to help. Police believe she played along with his fantasies in order to make hers a reality.

David, the adoring little brother, looked up to Jennifer as the one who cared for him. He shared her resentment at being at home alone so much, and he absorbed her anger at their mother, blaming Susan for something she could not help. Where Jennifer went David went, and he followed her into hell.

The difference between being seventeen and being fourteen is great at that age, and when Merrilee was accepted into the group, she basked in the attention of the older teens. Their games and ideas fascinated her, and she wanted to be a part of their alliance. Sex among the three of them brought them close, and she was so anxious to remain in their threesome that she would do anything to stay. When she believed that they were going to Canada without her she tried to stab her mother so she could take the car and get there before they left on the trip. Merrilee most likely would never have become violent without the influence of the others.

So four teens came together, and their combined needs created a perfect storm that killed Susan Bailey.

35

Where They Are Now

Susan Bailey died in September 2008 at the hands of her children, Jennifer and David Bailey, and her daughter's boyfriend, Paul Henson Jr. That event affected numerous lives in Roanoke, Texas, and in other locations around the United States. Some of the people most affected say that Susan's death changed their lives and they will never be the same.

Years have passed and life moves on, and in some ways so have the lives of the people who were most involved in the death and the investigation. But not everyone.

Richard Bailey visited his children while they were in the Denton County Jail and he visited Jennifer after she was transferred to the Gatesville Mountain View Unit. Kate and Stephen Morten continue to spend their summers in Minnesota and their winters in Arizona. They still are torn between their love of their grandchildren and their horror at what those children did to their daughter. Kate has tried to achieve closure with no success. She wants to move on and hopes that one day she can.

Texas Ranger Tracy Murphree's life changed drastically a few years afterward. His beautiful wife, Candace, was killed in an accident in downtown Sanger, Texas, leaving him with children, three of them under the age of nine. Murphree knew that he could not continue his career as a Ranger because of the long hours they work in all parts of Texas. He resigned from the Texas Department of Public Safety and took a job with the Denton County Sheriff's Office as a captain supervising the investigative bureau, the narcotics unit, crime-scene investigation and the SWAT team. In January 2015 Murphree left the sheriff's office and began working with a company that develops equipment for law enforcement officers and firefighters. In March of 2015 he announced his intention to run for sheriff of Denton County.

Investigator Larry Kish remains with the Denton County Sheriff's Office and has twice received promotions. He now serves as lieutenant over the investigative, narcotics, crime-scene and SWAT team aspects of the sheriff's office.

Roanoke Detective Brian Peterson left the department and moved closer to his home in South Texas. He now serves as chief deputy for the Somervell County Sheriff's Office. He is also co-owner of Heroes Cafe in Cleburne, Texas. The name honors law enforcement officers and firefighters.

Denton County Death Investigator Sharon Baughman now serves as lieutenant in the investigative bureau of the Cooke County Sheriff's Office in Gainesville, Texas.

Victoria Abbott remains chief of juvenile crimes prosecution for the Denton County District Attorney's Office.

Yankton Police Officer Eric Kolda left law enforcement in 2009 and owns a business in the private sector in Yankton.

Roanoke Police Chief Gary Johnson continues to serve as chief of the Roanoke Police Department. The town has settled back into being a low-crime area and the department has since not been forced to investigate anything as horrendous as the murder of Susan Bailey.

Jennifer Lucille Bailey remains in the Mountain View Unit of the Texas Department of Criminal Justice, serving a sixty-year sentence. Her first possible date of parole is September 26, 2038. She is considered indigent, with little financial help from family, and she subsists on the bare minimum the state is legally obligated to provide for prisoners.

David Lee Bailey is serving a twenty-six-year sentence and remains incarcerated at the Clemens Unit near Brazoria, Texas. He is working with a counselor to find a way to shorten the sentence because of his young age at the time of his crime, but at this time his first possible date for consideration of parole is October 1, 2021. He too is considered indigent.

Paul Allen Henson Jr. is serving a sixty-year sentence at the Mark W. Stiles Unit in Jefferson County near Beaumont, Texas. He receives visits from his father and stepmother and they contribute to his inmate account so that he can buy extra things like snacks and better clothing and shoes.

Merrilee White received a five-year probated sentence in the aggravated assault on her mother. She successfully completed that probation and now has no criminal record. The family moved out of the Northwest School District and she graduated from another high school, where no one knew about her past. She now is married with a baby and lives in a Metroplex city.

Susan's friends in The Parks at Roanoke and the friends she made at the businesses where she was working pause sometimes when she crosses their minds. Susan was an outgoing, hardworking, friendly woman who tried to take care of her children and did not deserve what her children did to her, the friends say.

Time Line

February 20, 1965—Susan Marie Morten* is born in Saint Paul, Minnesota.

March 1988—Susan Morten and Richard Bailey are married in California.

October 5, 1990—Jennifer Lucille Bailey is born in California.

October 6, 1994—David Lee Bailey is born in California.

December 27, 2006—Susan and Richard Bailey are legally divorced in Denton County, Texas.

September 23, 2008—Merrilee White is detained on a juvenile charge of aggravated assault after trying to stab her mother in Fort Worth, Texas.

September 26, 2008—Kate Morten calls Roanoke police because she can't reach her daughter, Susan Bailey. Officers ring the doorbell and no one answers.

September 27, 2008—Officers again go to house with no answer at the door.

September 28, 2008, 3:00 A.M.—Yankton Police Officer Eric Kolda finds the Bailey car with three teens inside and calls Roanoke police.

---

* Denotes pseudonym

September 28, 2008, 4:00 A.M.—Roanoke officers enter Bailey house and find Susan dead upstairs. They launch an investigation.

September 29, 2008—Texas Ranger Tracy Murphree, Denton County Investigator Larry Kish and Roanoke Detective Brian Peterson fly to South Dakota to search the Bailey car and try to talk to teens.

September 29, 2008—Autopsy is performed by Tarrant County medical examiner. Finding: Cause of death, numerous stab wounds to head and body. Manner of death, homicide.

October 1, 2008—Roanoke officers transport Jennifer and David Bailey and Paul Henson Jr. to Denton County Jail.

October 2, 2008—Memorial service takes place for Susan in Minnesota.

October 7, 2008—Fort Worth detention officers intercept letter from Merrilee White, aka "Doom Kitten," to Paul Henson Jr. and hand it over to Roanoke police. The letter implicates her in the conspiracy.

October 9, 2008—Memorial service for Susan in Texas.

December 11, 2008—Denton County grand jury issues indictments for capital murder for all three teens.

June 9, 2009—Paul Henson Jr. pleads guilty to murder in a plea agreement and is sentenced to sixty years in prison.

October 19, 2009—Jennifer Bailey pleads guilty to murder in a plea agreement and is sentenced to sixty years in prison.

October 28, 2009—David Bailey pleads guilty to murder in a plea agreement and is sentenced to twenty-six years, first in juvenile custody, and then in adult felony prison.

Afterword

I believe that a true-crime book contains the truth, not just the facts. Jack Webb, on the old *Dragnet* television program, used to ask for "Just the facts, ma'am." Newspaper reporters want the "who, what, why, when and how" of a story. But when I sit at my computer to write a true-crime book, I want to share the truth of the tale. I want readers to feel the love and the hatred that surround most murders and the frustration and determination of the law enforcement officers trying to solve them. I want them to see the setting in their mind's eye and smell the blood. And perhaps most important, I want readers to understand the why of the situation that led up to violent death. Sometimes that is the hardest part of all.

This story deals mostly with juveniles, and those youths have rights to privacy not accorded to adults. Texas lawmakers understand that immature youngsters sometimes do things—commit crimes—because they don't understand the gravity of the situation—like the "foreverness" of killing someone. Lawmakers want those youngsters to have another chance at making good decisions once they reach maturity. For that reason, the police files of juveniles are not public record.

Jennifer, at seventeen, was the only one of the four teens in this story to be considered an adult at the time of Susan Bailey's murder. All during the summer of 2014, I tried to obtain district attorney files to use to verify information I'd gotten from interviews. Letters from me to the Denton County district attorney, to the DA to the Texas attorney general and from the attorney general back to me crawled through the postal system. In the end, because of their status as juveniles, I was not able to obtain any files from David Bailey's case, nor from Paul Henson Jr.'s case, nor Tarrant County case files in the aggravated assault case against Merrilee White. But the case against Jennifer Bailey, a legal adult, was identical to those of David Bailey and Paul Henson Jr., so I was able to determine what had happened by using her files alone. When David and Paul reached the Texas Department of Criminal Justice, they had been declared adults and their prison information became public record but their earlier juvenile records did not.

I found witnesses who had known the teens and the victim and I probed their memories. Still, Jennifer, David and Paul, and to a lesser degree Merrilee, were the heartbeat of this story. Their voices needed to be heard if I, or anyone, was ever going to understand why this almost unthinkable crime was committed.

So I wrote to the three who were incarcerated asking for interviews, and I "friended" Merrilee on Facebook and asked to talk to her. The answers I received were mixed and a little confusing.

Merrilee was initially open to communicating with me. She got her second chance, she told me. Few people even know about the events of September 23, 2008, when her mother called Fort Worth police for help, and even fewer people realize that Merrilee was ever part of the conspiracy to kill Susan Bailey. She doesn't want anyone to find out. I promised that she would be given a pseudonym because of her juvenile status, and I continued to ask to talk to her. Finally, she agreed to meet me for an interview. We made an appointment and I drove to the city where she now lives, but she never arrived at the place where we had agreed to meet. Later I received a short, final note requesting that I talk to her lawyer if I had any other communication. Merrilee wanted to forget that she had ever plotted with three other teens to murder their parents.

For months I exchanged sporadic letters with Jennifer, David and Paul. Jennifer was afraid I would "twist her words and make her look bad." David would talk to me only if his sister did. Paul wondered what was in it for him.

I negotiated with them as best I could, agreeing that each of them would have a platform to tell his or her story without my judging or contradicting them. Finally, they agreed to be interviewed, and after negotiating dates and times with the public information officer of the Texas Department of Criminal Justice, I visited all three.

An Interview with Paul

The Mark W. Stiles Unit, where Paul Henson Jr. is incarcerated, has strong security. It lies on Farm to Market Road near Beaumont, and another prison unit and the sheriff's office and jail are located nearby. There is a guard shack at the front gate, where cars must stop before entering. A guard takes the driver's licenses of each person inside the car and checks them, most likely entering them into the Texas Crime Information Center system to make sure there are no outstanding warrants. In that event, the visitor would actually be taken into custody and placed in the nearby county jail.

After calling to make sure it is all right for me to enter, the guard gives an okay to proceed to the side of a long, institutional-looking building. There is a small building in front with a portico, and visitors enter there to be greeted by several guards and a metal-detection machine like those in an airport. A visitor must remove anything from pockets, plus jackets and shoes. The items are placed in a plastic box and run through the machine as visitors walk through the detector and then are patted down.

"Lift up your feet, one at a time," the guard instructs me.

I'm confused when I hear this strange order, so I stand on one foot and raise the other. The female guard looks at me like I'm stupid.

"No," she says. "I want to see the bottom of your feet."

She gestures for me to turn around, and I finally figure out that I must stand with my back to the guard and lift each foot to display the soles of my shoes. That accomplished, another guard behind a Plexiglas wall gestures me over and asks for my driver's license. She makes a copy of it, asks a few questions and passes it back through a small depression in the counter. She tells me to go outside through a back door, up a long sidewalk and into the building behind. Turn right and you will find the warden's office, she instructs.

Having done that and walking past two fences with concertina wire spread between them and then into a fairly normal looking building, I find the warden's office. Behind a desk sits a woman who smiles (the last smile I see inside the unit) and asks what my business here is. I tell her, and then she directs me down another long hall to a door. I stand before the door and hear the click as it is unlocked. Then I walk farther down the hall to another door, which also must be unlocked by an unseen guard. Outside large windows I see a big, half-covered patio with picnic tables protected by umbrellas. I walk past the second locked door and find myself in a "man trap" with another locked door on the other side. Another guard behind Plexiglas asks again for my driver's license.

Then nothing happens. The whole process so far has been confusing and unsettling. The guard ignores me. She keeps the driver's license. Through another door I can see a large room with tables and chairs and a long wall of Plexiglas with chairs on both sides where visitors can talk to inmates via telephones. Only two people are in the open room, a blonde woman writing on a legal pad and an inmate in the classic white uniform of prisoners in Texas. They are sitting at a table and talking together.

I don't know what to do. I'm being ignored by the busy guard behind the glass. Other people come up behind me and take things the guard shoves under the glass. These people are prison employees of some kind. They also ignore me, and I continue to grow more and more uncomfortable.

"What am I supposed to do?" I ask when I finally get the guard's attention.

"I don't know what to do with you," the guard replies. "I am trying to find out."

After more waiting, the guard nods at me and gestures toward the room with the blonde woman and the inmate.

"Go in there and sit down."

I do as I'm told. The blonde woman is not happy.

"I am supposed to be having a confidential visit," she says sharply.

"I'm sorry," I reply. "They told me to come in here."

After a few minutes, while I sit waiting, the blonde approaches the door and talks on a telephone there. The door opens and she goes into the man trap and speaks to someone. She returns and, shortly, another guard comes inside.

"You can't be in here," the guard says. "Go up there," she says with a vague gesture, "and get in one of those booths."

I comply, happy to escape the angry gaze of the blonde.

Inside the cubicle, I sit and wait to meet with Paul Henson Jr. The walls are made of flaking white plaster over concrete blocks. In front there is a scratched Plexiglas wall with a chair on the other side. Telephones hang from the side walls. Then comes the sound of the door to the cubicle unlocking, and Paul hobbles inside using a cane, and sets it against the wall. His hair is less than an inch long and he wears huge dark-framed glasses. Despite the owlish look the glasses give him, there still is something in his eyes that makes me grateful that he is locked into his side of the small cubicle.

The door locks behind him. He sits and we both pick up our telephones. But the phones are dead.

With no one visible to explain the problem to, we try to communicate by shouting and gesturing; it feels a bit like we are playing a game of charades. A few words come through but not enough to conduct an interview. Finally, I spot a guard and explain that we cannot communicate. The guard does not reply but disappears. She reappears on the inmate side and opens Paul's door. She gestures toward a grate in the concrete wall on the left side of Paul's wall. Then she shuts the door. Paul shouts and gestures that we will talk through that grate, but the door to the room on the other side of the grate is locked. I wait in frustration until the guard returns to my side of the wall and unlocks the door, then I pick up my chair and carry it into the nearly empty room. There's nothing in this room except a big plastic bag containing dozens of tennis shoes. I place my chair near the wall, which is one side of the cubicle where

Paul waits to talk to me, and bend over to reach the rusty metal grate. Paul and I cannot make eye contact now, but at least we can hear each other.

Paul knows that this is his chance to tell the world his story. I've offered him the opportunity to show his side. It is a window into his mind.

I ask about his cane, and Paul explains that he was injured when he fell from the second tier in a diagnostic unit near Huntsville, where he first was taken. (The second tier is akin to the second story of an apartment building. A second row of cells is stacked on top of the first tier of cells.) When he fell, he landed on his feet and both his heels were broken, he says. He doesn't explain how he came to fall, but he does say that he has attempted suicide a few times and shows scars on his arms from cuts. Several scars mark his arms. Some of those scars are from before he was incarcerated, when he cut himself to draw blood, he says. He was under a lot of stress as a teen, he says. That's why he cut himself. The flow of blood somehow relieved the stress that had built up. I recognize one of the scars on his arm from a photograph taken in Yankton, South Dakota.

The unit is currently on lockdown, he explains. Inmates stay locked inside their cells all day. No one is allowed to go to exercise or to the classes offered by the prison system. These general lockdowns happen a couple of times a year while guards routinely search for contraband. The lockdowns and searches may happen at any time for several reasons, Paul says. Because his visitor is a journalist with prior permission to interview him, he is allowed out of his cell.

He describes it. It is small, with room for bunk beds

against a wall, with lockers underneath for his property. There is a small table with two stools. There is a commode/sink combination. The cell has two Plexiglas windows to the outside, which open only two or three inches for fresh air. They are opaque and he can't see out.

He exercises and reads books from the library. He has earned his GED, or high school equivalency. He is allowed to attend religious services, and he chose Judaism. He likes the discipline of the religion, he says. There are scheduled library visits and scheduled times for the religious meetings. But the guards sometimes neglect to let him out of his cell for one of the visits. They don't much care one way or the other, he says.

So far, his description is not hard to believe. I've already seen how the guards smile and speak to one another, while inmates and visitors are handled seemingly without emotion or any attempt at humanity. It likely is the only way a guard can survive the work or carry out the job without becoming emotionally involved in some detrimental way. They apparently are trained to show no emotion, not to mention friendliness, to the inmates or their visitors. Still, it adds to the coldness of the atmosphere and contributes to the knowledge that the inmates are held against their wills and subject to the rules of a place they cannot leave. This, I believe, may be the worst aspect of incarceration. There is a total loss of humanity. I remind myself that Paul is here because he committed an atrocity.

This is an agricultural unit, but Paul cannot work because of his broken heels. It has been years at this point since he fell, and it appears that he will be crippled for the rest of his life.

There's a big tattoo on Paul's chest which reads, "Mind of a Maniac." He acquired it in prison. Paul says he suffers from deep depression and psychosis. He was diagnosed with it in the first unit he was sent to, one used to house prisoners until it is decided which unit the inmate will be sent to. He was prescribed medication for the psychosis and depression diagnosis, but the medication for that just makes him sleep, so he says he doesn't take it. He answers questions readily, and it is clear that he has formed his answers to the questions he expects will come and has gone over them in his mind. I did not send a list of questions ahead of time and I didn't even have a written list with which to conduct the interview. I wanted things to flow in a natural way.

Talos? He replies to one of my questions. Well, his other personality did exist, Paul says. Talos has not come out since he has been in prison, but he is sure that the other personality was real to him. He doesn't remember all that clearly, but Talos was part of his psychosis, he says now.

"I was seeing and hearing things that were not really there."

He explains that the *Demonic Bible* in his room at home wasn't really his—he says that he took that from a younger girl at school for her protection. She didn't realize that it was dangerous, and he didn't want her to get into trouble by reading it.

His dad and stepmother visit occasionally, and Paul Sr. puts money in his commissary account. His birth mother visited when he was in the diagnostic unit near Huntsville, but she has not been to the Stiles Unit.

Paul says he does not know why his parents divorced. He visited with his mother occasionally as a child.

Paul thinks about Jennifer a lot and hopes that she is doing well. If the murder had not happened, he believes they would have married. They could have been happy. There was a Walmart store close to his home and he could have found a job there. He hopes they can get together after both are released. He received a couple of letters from her at first, but he hasn't heard from her in years, he says. He never heard from David.

Paul explained about hiding in Jennifer's house. There were several good hiding places inside, or sometimes, when he heard the garage door going up, he would slip out the back door and head to the park across the street. It was easy to hide in the park in good weather.

Merrilee was a nice girl and he enjoyed hanging out with her, but he had no idea she planned to kill her mother, he says. He was shocked when he heard that she had tried to stab her mother. There had been no conspiracy to kill their parents, and he had had no intention of shooting his father and stepmother.

Yes, he and Jennifer had a plan, but it hadn't included killing her mother, Paul says. They were planning to save up cash and travel to Canada eventually. He needed to get a driver's license first. He only had a learner's permit at the time. Jennifer wanted to obtain legal custody of David so that they could take him along. The gun he stole from his father was only for protection.

Paul's answers are careful.

The night that Susan Bailey died, he says he planned to talk to her. He says that he wanted to apologize for the trouble he had caused, and he wanted to ask her if Jennifer could come to live with him. Then he planned to go home and ask his parents if Jennifer could come to live at their house. He wanted to finish his high school education before anything else happened. He thought everything was going to be all right, Paul says. But when Susan got home everything changed.

Paul's version of events differs greatly from others I've heard so far. He said that Jennifer was in her room when they heard Susan arrive, and he was in the game room. Susan walked up the stairs and went to Jennifer's door. They began to argue. Then David emerged from his room, wielding a knife.

"When everything went down, I couldn't fathom what I was seeing. I was shocked. David walked out of his room holding a big knife. Me nor Jennifer knew what to do. We didn't know he was going to do that and we didn't know why. It was panic," he said. "We made an erratic decision based on panic. None of us made the right choice. If we had been more mature . . ."

David acted alone; they had no plan to kill Susan. Her thirteen-year-old son was the one who stabbed her over and over, while Paul and Jennifer watched in amazement. When Susan was dead, they simply panicked and had no idea what they should do. Finally, they took off in Susan's car with almost no money. They drove across the country without a plan, and they ran out of money and gasoline in Yankton.

They didn't bring the stabbing up on the trip, Paul says. They were all too nervous and upset. He drove and nobody said much.

"I regret panicking. I regret my choice of actions. We would not be in the predicament we are in now."

Paul is adamant that he and Jennifer are innocent of anything except running away after David killed his mother. Their lives are ruined because of something neither of them knew was about to happen.

He says that he signed the confession "against my will" under duress and the effects of the medication he was given.

"I could have beaten this case if it had gone to trial. It was all hearsay. Both of us are here on hearsay. I should have been more my age."

Paul says his DNA was on the electrical cord because he was using it to show David how electricity works. That is the way his dad taught him about electricity, he said. He frayed the wires and showed the boy which wire did what thing. That's all that cord was about, he states. He has no idea how it came to be wrapped around the doorknob in the bathroom, strung across the shower curtain rod and dangling near the water in the tub. It was some kind of setup, he believes.

Paul has been in prison for six years already and is facing many, many more. It will be thirty years before there will be a parole hearing to determine "if I am fit to be integrated back into society," Paul says. He does not expect to be released the first time he comes up for parole. But he thinks about getting Jennifer released all the time.

"I would like to get a lawyer to exonerate her. She is innocent."

Jennifer was so good for him. She helped him so much. She helped him with the stress so that he didn't cut himself so much. The stress was from his adolescence. It's hard to be a teenager, and his life was stressful. He and Jennifer were in love and he hopes they will have the chance to have a life together some day.

"Myself and her are completely innocent. It was all hearsay. If we are going to speak on hearsay, there's no reason to speak on anything. I am only a threat to myself."

I left Paul and the prison unit with an unsettled feeling. The atmosphere had not been pleasant. I had not believed some of the answers to my questions. And after two hours of being locked inside a big, utterly sterile building, I was desperate for a kind word and a smile.

An Interview with David

Gone is the cherubic face, the goofy grin of a thirteen-year-old kid mugging for the camera. Here, in a rusty-redbrick building built in 1893 as a prison for black criminals, sits a composed nineteen-year-old boy who could have been perched on any chair anywhere talking about sports or cars or nineteen-year-old girls.

When it was built, segregation of prisoners, as in all other aspects of life, mandated that black inmates be housed separately from their equally guilty white brothers and sisters. So in 1890 William Clemens, chairman of the Texas Prison Board at that time, bought five thousand five hundred acres near the tiny town of Brazoria.

The unit remained all-black until the prison system was integrated in the mid-1970s. After that it was an all-male prison unit without age requirements until the mid-1990s, when older offenders were moved to other units and inmates under twenty-five replaced them. It became colloquially known as the "kiddie farm."

David Bailey has been here for more than a year, since he turned eighteen in a Texas Juvenile Justice Department facility and was transferred to "big-boy prison," as the move from juvenile to adult incarceration is sometimes called.

David does not show any signs of having grown up in prison. Intelligence and sincerity shine out of his eyes, and his ears look slightly too big because of his close-cropped hair. He looks like a kid you'd like to take to a baseball game.

But David Bailey is doing twenty-six years for murder. And out of three teens who participated in a stabbing in 2008, he is the only one who says he is sorry, so sorry, for what he did.

The Clemens Unit lies on the coastal plains in Brazoria County, south of Houston, so close to the Gulf of Mexico that inmates swear they hear the seabirds crying at sunrise. Nearby resort towns offer sand and seashells and waves breaking gently on beaches with soft sighs.

But inmates at Clemens don't see the ocean or anything pretty. That is not their world. Their world is the Clemens Unit of the Texas Department of Criminal Justice. Their world is an ugly, low-tech kind of building, which is showing its age. They work on the prison farm raising crops and vegetables and some cattle. Even the concertina wire stacked between the fences in the no-man's land between them and the outside world is blackened with age and bent out of its perfect coil.

I take in the bare landscape and ugly brickwork one morning on the way to talk to David about his crime and his present surroundings. I stand at the foot of a tall guard tower next to a man who also is making a case for getting inside. Sometimes it seems like it must be as hard to get inside the prison as to get out, though that is really not true. The guard in the tower is confused as she lowers a plastic bin on a rope on the morning of January 7, 2015.

"Just put your driver's license in there," she says, and begins hauling the bin back up to the platform. "Now, what was it you said you were doing here?"

The pleasant-looking man stands by watching. He is also waiting for the guard to figure out what to do with him.

"I come here once a week. I am part of the faith-based program," he explains to me. "Most of the guards know me, but this one doesn't."

"It seems like every unit does things differently. This one is very different from the one I was in yesterday," I tell him.

"This one is different every week," he says.

Finally, after a few more telephone calls, the guard allows the man to enter the gate. Then she turns her attention back to me.

"You say you are public media? Where are you supposed to go?"

"I have no idea," I reply. "I'm here to interview an inmate is all I know."

"Okay," the guard finally says, lowering the plastic bin with my driver's license inside. "Just go on in. When you get inside that first gate, hold your driver's license up to the camera."

So I'm admitted through two locked gates and a locked door to an anteroom with a metal detector, an officer who performs a pat-down and more confused employees.

"And what are you doing here?" a male guard asks.

"She has a camera. She can't have a camera in here, can she?" a female guard insists.

"I brought one into Stiles yesterday," I say, and finally the guard drops her objections.

And so the explanations begin again, until at last I am directed down a hallway and told to turn right, enter the big room and take any seat I want. I find a familiar-looking visitation room with long rows of barriers and chairs with room on both sides for inmates and their loved ones. The room is empty.

I sit and wait. And wait, inspecting the forlorn couch pushed against a rusty-red wall, a potato chip machine, the yellowed white linoleum floor. After twenty minutes, I venture back to the anteroom.

"Uh, no one has come yet," I tell a friendly guard.

"What? Oh. I'll take care of it," he replies. "You just go back and sit down and he'll be there in a minute."

This unit feels a little more human than the Stiles Unit I visited yesterday. I figure it is because only young offenders are housed here, and few of them have committed the kind of crime David did. In a few minutes David walks in, smiling hesitantly. He is wearing his white prison uniform and a black jacket. Even in South Texas, it is a cold day.

In this place, the barrier is not Plexiglas but wire mesh. Talking is easy, and there is a feeling of intimacy not present in the other facilities. A guard seats himself about halfway down the room, giving the two of us a feeling of privacy. We begin to talk, slowly getting to know each other. He works in the kitchen serving food, David explains. His shift starts at one A.M. and he works until six or seven A.M. Then he goes back to his dorm. An inmate's day begins early, and work starts soon after breakfast. The point, I believe, is to reach the evening with tired, sleepy men or women who don't have the energy to start trouble and are willing to go to bed.

The dormitory is a large room currently occupied by thirty-six young men, but it could house twice that number, he says. The room contains cubicles with beds, but the inmates have the big room to walk around in, and there obviously is more freedom here than in more restrictive facilities.

David attends a faith-based program four nights a week. On Wednesdays, he attends a Toastmasters club for an hour and a half. The training shows in David's well-spoken, easy demeanor. But it isn't just about speaking; it's about communicating, he says. He enjoys the program. He also participates in a praise and worship band. There he plays the trombone, which he started learning to use as a child in middle school. And he is a backup singer, he says with a smile.

David is able to call his paternal aunt when she has placed funds in his account to do so. She is his only contact with the outside world. His father visited when he was still in Denton County but he has not been to see him since. His dad is unemployed, without a car, David explains, and the woman he lives with has not set up their telephone so that he can receive prepaid calls from prison. David does receive letters from Jennifer, and they are his lifeline.

"I'd like to get a pen pal," he says. "But it is really complicated without the Internet, and we don't have that. So there are these lists you can go through, but I don't have a pen pal yet."

He has hopes of shortening his sentence through a "time

cut" program. He sends his "good time" record and any other detail that might show him in a good light with letters to Denton County. The judge who sentenced him, the district attorney and the sheriff have a chance to recommend that his sentence be shortened. He hopes that because of his behavior record and his age when he was sentenced, they will agree.

David had at first written to me that he could not remember the night of the murder at all. He said that he wanted to remember—the people who were working with him wanted him to as well. It would be healthy for him to remember so he could deal with it. Now, though, he says it is coming back to him. His memories mirror Jennifer's.

"A lot of my life is a little hazy," he begins. "But I remember my house. I can even remember the layout in perfect detail. But I am lacking in distinct memories. I got help for it in TYC," the Texas Youth Commission facility he was in until he turned eighteen. "They have to check what I say against information they have. I honestly don't remember how I got involved in this, but I was."

Three things happened to him in the two years preceding his mother's murder, he explains. First, his best friend moved away. Then his parents divorced. And then his grandfather on his father's side, the man who took care of him from infancy until they moved to Texas, died. All that piled up on him, and he was depressed. He no longer wanted to get close to anyone. It seemed like people he loved just went away. He stopped doing his homework and his grades fell.

"Mom was working all the time. I kind of felt cheated.

Now I appreciate what she did for me. Growing up I had everything I wanted because of her, but I had a spoiled-brat mentality."

His sister, Jennifer, was the one constant in his life. There was a strong bond between them, and she was like a mother to him.

"That bond was the reason why everything happened. I was afraid of losing my sister. I had self-esteem problems, and I still have self-esteem problems. I made decent grades before, but then they were bad. I was learning in class and could pass the tests but I just didn't turn in any homework."

David never really understood why his parents divorced. His father got mad and yelled a lot, he recalls. Once his parents were fighting so badly that police arrived. His mother packed her bags and told David that she was leaving but she would be back. The next thing he remembers is his dad moving out.

"I have some anger issues. The TYC psychologist said I over-controlled my emotions."

Then Jennifer started dating Paul and she and their mom argued constantly over him. Susan didn't like him. She said he was weird.

"I thought he was weird too, but at the same time I thought *I* was weird. Our views of ourselves were very similar. We were sad, depressed, angry. My anger became a monster. I fought it, but it was stronger. I let the monster out. I believed I was a werewolf, and I viewed myself as a monster."

Faith in God saved David, he believes. He now is a child of God, and in His grace David, he says, is perfect.

"It's mind-boggling that He would give me His love. Now I look at my faith group as a family. They are my family. They are people I can trust."

He says he was never really a cutter. He just saw the scars on Paul's arms and decided to try it himself. He cut his arm, and it hurt.

"I thought, 'I am never doing this again.' I'm not a pain freak."

He brought the knife to school that day to look cool, to show off. A friend of his got the knife and argued with another boy. His friend tried to stab the other boy, and the school authorities found out. He was in trouble, received in-school suspension. When his mother asked him why he brought the knife to school, he says, "I lied. I said there were some boys at school threatening me. But really, I was just showing off."

David didn't know much about Merrilee, though he does recall that she was hiding in their house for a while. Jennifer had put a blanket and pillow in the narrow space between her bed and the wall, and that's where Merrilee slept. One day she left to go to the store and never returned. He didn't know that she was discovered walking down the street and taken home by her mother and that she tried to stab her mother the next morning, he says. One of the detectives told him what happened to Merrilee after he returned to Denton, and it answered some questions about the girl for him.

The pudding incident was bigger than the police realized, according to David. Jennifer and Merrilee had crushed up a whole bottle of Tylenol and put it in the chocolate pudding. The intent was for it to put Susan to sleep, and then David would kill her, they'd decided.

"The plan was I would go in and stab her. I picked out one of the biggest knives. I checked the route from my room to hers for squeaks in the floor. I marked out each step I would take. But then she took one bite and said it tasted bad. So when she went to sleep that night I just got up and went to her room. I was standing over her with a knife in my hand. I was blank. Just empty. I had no thoughts. But then one thought came to me—'I can't do this.' I walked out."

David went downstairs and into the kitchen pantry, where Jennifer was waiting.

"I just broke down crying. I said I couldn't do it. She hugged me and said it was OK. Then Mom walked into the kitchen and said, 'What are you doing?' We said, 'Nothing' and she told us to go back to bed."

David remembers when officers came and searched the house for Paul. He had been there, but he somehow disappeared and the police didn't find him. It was a strange, unreal time and hazy in his memory.

The teens devised another plan to kill Susan. David went to the store, he said, and bought bleach and Windex, though the store receipt shows he actually bought Formula 409. He bought safety glasses, he said. He put them on and mixed the chemicals together in a plastic bag in the backyard. He put a cloth inside the bag to soak it in the chemicals. That night they were going to hold the cloth over Susan's mouth to make her pass out. Then they were going to stab her and drag her to the tub and throw the cord in with her. All that should kill her, they thought.

All that day, he, Jennifer and Paul played on the Internet to pass time. When it got close to when Susan would return home, he and Paul went to the game room and David sat cross-legged on the floor and meditated. Paul sprawled on the floor. Then they heard the garage door going up. David went to his room and Paul crouched behind the wall of the game room next to the stairs. David put on the bandana to protect him from the chemicals on the rag. He had a knife in his pocket, he said.

"I had the feeling that I couldn't do it. I took off the bandana. I'm thinking, 'When it goes down, I'm gonna run away.'"

As Susan topped the stairs, Paul had a big knife and Jennifer had the small baseball bat. David was scared. He went back into his room. He could hear his mother screaming, he said.

"I froze. I was just stuck. Not even breathing. She stopped screaming and I opened the door and went out and saw her on the floor. There was blood pooling and Jennifer was crying. There was no doubt that she was dead. I just burst into tears too. Jennifer ran into the bathroom and was throwing up. Paul told me to hold her hair so she wouldn't get vomit in it, and I did. Paul told us to be careful and not to step in blood."

David doesn't remember anyone washing up, despite the forensic evidence that someone washed off blood in both bathtubs and the powder room downstairs. He just doesn't recall that, he says. They all ran downstairs, taking nothing with them. They forgot to look for cash or to bring any clothing with them. They were in a panic.

"We were all crying. Paul kept apologizing. I told him it needed to be done. I was telling him that so that I wouldn't have to feel bad about it."

They piled into Susan's car, taking the basset hound, Ginger, and the cat with them. They drove away with Paul at the wheel. The first night they pulled into a truck-stop parking lot and slept in the car. They existed on beef jerky. At some point, Paul discovered that he had blood on his sleeve and on a sock. He told them that if anyone noticed, they were to say there had been a hunting accident.

They had Susan's ATM card and tried to use it but they did not know her passcode. They needed money in the worst way.

"We begged," David said. "We came up with a story about visiting our dad in Iowa. We were young and sad and people gave us money. At one point, Paul shoplifted a bone and gave it to the dog."

They had no money to feed the cat, so they left it on the side of a road, he said. The next night they found an empty parking lot and David let down the backseat so he could stretch out. He slept and dreamed. Part of his dream seemed to be about the dog, which also was dreaming, he thought. He awoke, frightened. The dog had been scared. Animals could sense when bad things were going to happen, David says. He woke Jennifer and told her that something bad was coming. She told him to go back to sleep.

Later that night they got back on the road. They were nearly out of gas when they stopped at the station in Yankton, South Dakota. They were trying the pumps to see if one of them might work when they saw the police car pull in.

"We were going to try to play it off. But we had no driver's licenses and no insurance card with us. He talked to us and then I saw him talking on his radio and then three vans pulled up. They put us in the three vans."

David remembers that he and Paul were "messing around" in one of the cars while en route back home to Texas, and remarks that his recorded words made it seem like he was not remorseful enough. (The recording he refers to is the one of him talking to Paul about sending his dead mother's body to the zoo and giggling.) That worked against him when he was sentenced, David says.

He remembers seeing Paul stabbing his mother. He remembers seeing Jennifer staring into the mirror after she threw up. She was having second thoughts, he believes, but it was much too late.

But, having worked with psychologists at the juvenile facility, he has learned so much since that time, David says now. He's learned that he was wrong when he thought his mother didn't love him.

"In my mind, she hadn't been there for me. Now I realize that she had always been there. If I had sat down and thought about it, I would have realized how stupid I was. But I didn't. I was too immature.

"Words can't express how sorry I am," David says. "I made a choice and that choice was wrong. Nothing will ever excuse it. I have learned to appreciate what I had. Mom loved me so much. Sometimes, you don't know what you have until you lose it and can't ever get it back."

An Interview with Jennifer

The Mountain View Unit of the Texas Department of Criminal Justice lies on State School Road, just to the north of Texas State Highway 36 between the small Central Texas towns of Hamilton and Gatesville. The countryside is pretty, with trees and rolling hills.

This unit houses only women, including women on death row. The campus is large, with numerous buildings. There are several other prison units near Gatesville, and many townspeople hold jobs in the prisons as guards or other staff. The prison system is the chief employer for the whole area.

Mountain View, like all the other prison units, is surrounded by fences festooned with concertina wire, which also is known as razor wire, and for a good reason. It is impossible to touch the wire anywhere without being cut. Two fences surround the unit, separated by a distance of about ten feet blanketed with rough white rocks, and each fence has coils of the concertina wire stacked from the ground nearly to the top and another roll attached to the top. Anyone attempting to climb either of those fences would be cut everywhere and could even bleed to death.

Interspersed along the fences are guard towers, each with a guard watching that segment of the grounds. A few inmates, always escorted by a guard, can be seen moving among the buildings behind the fence in their white uniforms. Visitors are instructed not to wear white clothing when they visit. The absence of trees and shrubbery allows few outdoor places to hide. Locked gates give access only to authorized people with keys. It is a forbidding landscape.

Visitors are patted down for contraband. No cell phones are allowed inside. Once through the concertina wire and the gates, it is a short walk to a free-standing building that is a visitor's center, where a key must be used to unlock the door. The center consists of three main rooms and a separate room for attorney visits. Friends and relatives may visit in this center but are not allowed in the other facilities on the grounds. First comes a lobby for visitors to wait at tables in a room with toilets and vending machines. Through another locked door lie two other long, narrow rooms outfitted with chairs and a clear plastic divider with a shelf along their lengths. In the middle is a third area where inmates sit in chairs facing out into each room. The thick plastic barrier precludes touching between visitors and inmates. Telephones are provided so the inmate and visitor can talk privately, but there is also a grate that allows conversation without the phone. Some people don't want to use the telephones because there is a rumor that guards listen in on the conversations.

At the end of the room, a guard sits watching and listening behind a metal screen.

Jennifer Bailey, now twenty-four years old, sits on the inmate side of the barrier. Outside, beautiful sunshine and mild temperatures make it a day perfect for being outdoors, but Jennifer has little chance to enjoy the weather even through a window. She has been placed at the far end of the room next to the guard station with a view of the blank inside of the outer wall of the building. She carries a few tissues with her and nothing else. There have been lengthy negotiations before this meeting. She understands that while I am writing about the killing of Susan Bailey using police reports and interviews with officers who worked the case, this will be a chance for her to tell her story—her words, unchallenged. This is her opportunity to convince people not to judge her so harshly.

Jennifer sits in her chair wearing her white prison uniform and looking eager, smiling. Her light brown hair is shorter than it was when she was captured—it's now a little above her shoulders—and she wears it pulled back into a ponytail. Even without makeup, Jennifer is pretty, and her smile is sweet. Her expression is open and her eyes hold intelligence, curiosity and some hope. I am her first visitor in more than two years.

Jennifer's day begins at three thirty, she says. She arises, dresses and has breakfast. At four fifteen A.M. she is allowed entry to the laundry room, where she uses her small allotment of soap to wash her clothing. Jennifer is classified as indigent. Although her father's sister occasionally sends a little cash to both Jennifer's and David's accounts as often as she can afford it, Jennifer usually has no one to put money into her commissary account, where she could purchase more than the meager monthly allotment of soap. Indigent inmates are given small amounts of shampoo, body soap and other necessities. They are not given hair conditioner, lotion or any things many people consider the necessities of life. Jennifer misses those things and would buy them if she could.

She has been, in practical matters, excommunicated from her mother's side of the family. Her father lives in Irving, Texas, nearly a hundred and fifty miles away. His sister is retired, and cannot make a trip from California to visit. It is too far and too expensive to travel.

At five thirty A.M. Jennifer reports to her job on the prison campus. She transcribes textbooks into Braille to be used by the Texas School for the Blind and Visually Impaired, a school that offers an education for blind and visually impaired people up to the age of twenty-one as well as resources for parents of blind children.

Jennifer uses her artistic talent to draw charts and graphs for the schoolbooks. She is compiling a portfolio that she hopes to use after her eventual release to become employed by the school and continue to work for the program from home. She would draw a small salary. Reading and translating the textbooks gives her a chance to learn as well. Some of the textbooks are at college level. Jennifer would love to take the college classes offered on campus and at a nearby college. She would not be allowed off campus to attend the college because of the severity of her crime, but even though there are some college classes offered on campus, she says that inmates have to pay tuition for those classes, and she cannot.

Jennifer is proud of the work she does for the Braille program. Recently the women in her unit received a commendation for being the best prison facility in the state in the Braille program.

"We got some positive feedback. Some of us cried when they told us," she said.

At eleven thirty A.M. she leaves the computer facility and goes back to her unit to eat lunch. Noon until two P.M. is recreation time, and she recently joined the volleyball team. (Again, however, because of her violent criminal status, she is not allowed to leave the campus for tournaments at other units.) After rec, she returns to her unit and naps until dinnertime at five P.M., Jennifer says. After dinner, she is allowed to draw or socialize with other inmates until bedtime.

Jennifer's sixty-year sentence allows for a parole hearing after thirty years. But years are counted by adding real time served to "good time" earned. Jennifer earns good time by working and by going through self-help programs offered by the prison system on campus. She stays out of trouble. That good time accrues but cannot be used to shorten her sentence. It does show on her record, and she hopes to write the letters to the judge, the district attorney and the sheriff to ask for a shorter sentence. In this "time cut" program, they will consider her crime and her record in prison. If at least two of them agree, she could earn a shorter sentence. She has hopes to trim years from her sentence, and she is bent on getting out early.

"I'm not miserable here," she says. "But I do miss my family. I wish I could just go home right now. We don't give up hope. I have not given up. I will go home when God decides it is time for me to go home."

Jennifer states that she entered the Mountain View Unit with a willingness to change. And she believes she has changed. She found God in the Denton County Jail, and she goes to church services regularly and studies the Bible.

"When they walked into my pod [in county jail] with the indictment papers, I knew I was going to do time. I knew I had to change. I was dead inside. Now I am not. I am dedicated to my Lord. I have taken every program that I can to help me change."

She has not seen her brother, David, in six years—not since they left South Dakota. She misses him terribly. She acted as a mother figure to David, and they were close. Now they can send regular letters to each other. If he is paroled early from his twenty-six-year sentence, he might be able to visit her. But at this point, any visit would be at least seven years down the road. And there is no guarantee that he *will* be paroled.

"Growing up, we only had each other," she said. "That's the way we felt."

Even though she knew why Susan was absent so much, she resented having to be a mother to her little brother, Jennifer admits. Susan always had been particular about her house, and she expected her daughter to keep it clean.

"Nobody knew what went on behind closed doors," she comments, saying, "Once she came to the school and pulled me out of class and took me home and made me clean the house all day until one A.M. I had left dirty dishes, and she just took me out of school and made me wash them and then the whole rest of the house from top to bottom."

She and David finally rebelled, Jennifer says. They didn't argue, but they didn't clean. They only did the minimum they could get away with. That's why the house was in such a mess the day Susan died. They had simply stopped doing as they were told about the housework, she explains.

She acknowledges that her mother worked constantly, often holding two jobs. When they were in California, they'd lived with their fraternal grandparents, who loved them and took care of them while Susan and Richard Bailey worked. Her dad usually had a job back then, she remembers. He went to truck driving school and was a long-distance trucker for a short time.

But once they moved to Texas, Richard attended a technical college. After her mother filed for divorce, she says, he moved to Iowa and was employed at a hospital working on heart monitors. When he returned to Texas, he was hired by an oil rig company, where he worked for a while repairing the big drilling rigs.

Her father never hit her or David, but he did yell at them. So did their mother, she said. Susan called David stupid.

Jennifer says that she came to distrust her parents. She tells me that a friend of her father's began molesting her when she was thirteen, and although she told both Susan and Richard, neither of them believed her. The improper touching lasted three years, with her staying quiet because she knew she would not be believed. Finally, she decided that he was not going to touch her again and she told him that she would tell police if he molested her again. And he stopped.

About three months before her death, Susan had a talk with Jennifer. She wanted to know why the girl had been angry at her for so long. So Jennifer spoke once more about the molestation that Susan had discounted. She told her mother that she resented having to take care of David, and that both of them resented having to clean the house. Her mother told her that she would try to be a better mother to them both, Jennifer recalls. She did try. Jennifer could tell that she was trying to be the mother that Jennifer wanted. But she still had to work the long hours to keep food on the table. She wanted to sell the house but the market was down and it didn't sell, Jennifer said. Her mother seemed desperate for money all the time, and Jennifer still had to be a mother to her brother. That part didn't change.

"I had no social life. I couldn't go anywhere because I had to stay with him."

She was close to her father's parents until the family moved to Texas when she was eight years old. She didn't see much of her mother's parents during her growing-up years and felt that they were rigid, much like her own mother. They seemed disapproving to her, just as Susan disapproved of their housekeeping. She and David never were able to clean to her satisfaction, and that was the reason they just stopped trying, Jennifer says.

She met Paul at Northwest High School. He wasn't handsome, but he fascinated her. He was different from other boys, dark and mysterious like the heroes of some of the fantasy books she read. He used to stare at her, so finally she walked up and introduced herself. They started hanging out together and before long they became inseparable. She liked to hear about the strange, foreign worlds he inhabited in his fantasies. Paul claimed to have a split personality, and she believed him.

"When he became Talos, there was a shift. His eyes changed. He wasn't Paul," she says.

She was curious about all the things he was into, like Wicca and reincarnation and believing in demons. She read about Wicca and in a casual way practiced the belief. She wasn't a formal follower of the practice of white witchcraft, but it was something that drew her to learn more. They played their fantasy games, which became more weird and violent as time wore on.

"I was intrigued. Curious. I have a scientific mind, and I wanted to know what made him tick. I don't have that kind of curiosity anymore. I don't want to ever have anything more to do with him."

She and Paul had a lot of things in common, she believed. They both were unhappy with their home life. Paul didn't talk about it though.

She and Merrilee didn't fight about Paul/Talos. Both of them really believed that those were two different people inside the same body. She did not know, she says, that Merrilee was planning to stab her mother. She denies that they planned that together.

"I'll be honest. I didn't even think that Paul would do that. I thought it was just something we talked about. I never even thought it would really happen."

Killing Susan was Paul's idea, she insists. He didn't like

the things he heard Jennifer say about her unhappiness with her home life, and the things she was forced to do because her mother worked so hard. And her mother didn't like him either and tried to keep them from seeing each other. Paul wanted her mother dead. He called Jennifer on the telephone one day and told her that this was what they were going to do: they were going to kill Susan Bailey. David knew about the plan because he heard them talking, she said.

"But we didn't wish that on our mother. We didn't do it. I never told anybody that we didn't know it was going to happen. We did. But we didn't stab her. That was our crime. Knowing and not telling."

The night of the murder, Jennifer and David waited up for their mother downstairs while Paul waited upstairs in the game room, she said. Susan had told them they were to hand over their cell phones when she got home. She was taking the cell phones away because they had run up a $1,700 bill the first month, Jennifer recalls, insisting that they had had no idea they were overusing the telephone pay plan. They didn't understand how it worked. She believes that her mother came into the house about one thirty A.M. as the night turned into Friday. She doesn't remember when David went up to his room. She went upstairs and went into the hall bathroom, she said. Then she heard her mother scream.

"I ran into the hall and Paul had her up against the wall with a knife to her throat. I yelled for him to stop, and Mom was yelling for me to call the police. I said no."

But then, Jennifer says, she ran to a telephone and tried to call 911.

"He said, 'Put the phone down.' I did. Then he cut her

throat. I saw it happen. I was frozen in place. It's like it was a dream. It wasn't real. But I didn't stab her and neither did David. He came out of his room and just broke down crying."

She watched her mother die of multiple stab wounds but she and David just watched in horror, she says. Jennifer was surprised to learn that there was evidence of people washing a lot of blood away in both bathrooms and the small toilet downstairs. She said none of them bathed. She only had a small amount of blood on one leg from where it sprayed on her, she insists. After the attack, they all climbed into Susan's car and fled.

"I can't prove that David and I ran just because we were scared, but that's why we did," Jennifer said. "I wish I could forget what happened. I do. It was horrible."

Jennifer denies ever telling anyone that she hit her mother with the small baseball bat. She says she mixed the bottle of pills into the pudding to make her mother sleep. Susan ran on adrenaline. She never got enough rest or enough sleep.

"I thought if she went to sleep she would get some rest. That's all that was," the girl said.

She says that she was actually glad when the South Dakota officer stopped them that early Sunday morning. They had no real plan for what they would do next and no money, and she didn't want to spend the rest of her life on the run.

She has made her peace and asked forgiveness from God for what she did that night, Jennifer says. She believes that God has forgiven her.

She misses her mother every day and wishes that she had not died. She would change that if she could, Jennifer says, and as she speaks, tears run down her cheeks. She reaches for the tissues she brought along.

"I was hurt, but that didn't mean I didn't love her. I can tell you that if she had not died, something would have happened. I couldn't handle it anymore. I would have snapped."

The guard sitting behind a screen signals that it is time for Jennifer to go back to her unit. But first she has some last words for people who know what happened and would judge her.

"I don't want to stay in here forever. I want to see my family. I want people to know that I'm doing everything I can to not be the person I was when I came in here. I have changed. I am a better person. I am rehabilitated. I want to go home."

Jennifer does not seem to realize that, for the Bailey family, there no longer is a "home." The house went into foreclosure and a bank reclaimed it. Years passed with the house sitting empty on its lot on Oxford Drive. The bank sent workers to tear out all the carpet and repaint. Doors were replaced and walls were patched. Texas law mandates disclosure of a murder in a house when it is for sale. It didn't sell fast. But finally a new family bought the house and moved in. It had been a house of horror for Susan. It was clean and new and a harbinger of a bright future for the new owners. The neighbors didn't talk to them about the people who had lived there before.

The home and family that Jennifer cries for at night don't exist anymore. Her brother is incarcerated hundreds of miles away. Her father has no job and no car and lives with a woman Jennifer has never met. Her mother's side of the family wants nothing to do with her. If she ever is released, there is no home for her to go back to.

A guard comes to escort me back out the door, and locks it behind him. We walk past the concertina wire and through two locked gates. I am free to walk in the thin December sunshine and drive away from the prison.

Jennifer stays inside.

Author's Note

Kate and Stephen Morten are not the real names of Susan Bailey's parents. They have not been able to come to grips with the awful facts of this case and asked that their names be changed for this book. With thanks for their help, sympathy for their plight and respect for their privacy, I granted their wish.

The names of Merrilee White and her parents, Amy and Shane White, were also changed, to protect the legal privacy of a juvenile.